P9-CRT-660

Teaching Media Skills

Teaching
Media Skills

An Instructional Program
for Elementary and Middle School Students

H. Thomas Walker
Supervisor of Media Services
Howard County Public School System
Clarksville, Maryland

Paula Kay Montgomery
Teacher Specialist
Department of Educational Media
and Technology
Montgomery County Public Schools
Rockville, Maryland

LIBRARIES UNLIMITED, INC.
Littleton, Colorado

1977

LIBRARIES UNLIMITED, INC.
P.O. Box 263
Littleton, Colorado 80160

Library of Congress Cataloging in Publication Data

Walker, H   Thomas, 1944-
    Teaching media skills.

    Bibliography: p. 161
    Includes index.
    1. School children--Library orientation.
2. Instructional materials centers. I. Montgomery,
Paula Kay, joint author. II. Title.
Z675.S3W2   027.62'5   76-30605
ISBN 0-87287-135-5

TABLE OF CONTENTS

PART III—BIBLIOGRAPHY OF INSTRUCTIONAL MATERIALS FOR MEDIA SKILLS, 161

PART IV—LIST OF VENDORS, 181

PREFACE

For as long as school libraries have been called "media centers," there has been discussion in the journal literature of school librarianship regarding the instructional role of the media specialist. The conceptualization of that role has proceeded from early discussion of "library orientation" (early 1960s and before), through the notion of "supporting classroom instruction" (late 1960s), to the current description of the school media specialist as an active participant in the instructional planning process, a supporting participant in everyday instruction, and the school staff member charged with primary responsibility for teaching research, communication, and media skills.

A concurrent trend in the literature of education has been a move toward the empirical rationalization of the teaching process. In the empirical, or "behavioral" view, the teacher is held accountable for the learning of students and is therefore required to base instructional methodology on a series of precise objectives stated in terms of student behavior ("behavioral" or "instructional objectives"). Since the accomplishment of objectives stated in behavioral terms may be easily observed in students, the effectiveness of the teacher and the teaching process is thereby easily demonstrable.

Since 1958, many of the foremost spokesmen of school librarianship—John Gillespie, Richard Darling, James Liesener, Eleanor Ahlers, and others—have urged the integration of library or media skills instruction into the classroom teaching process. Scarcely a single professional meeting or conference passes without discussion of the issue, and several of the most prominent school systems in the country have established systematic programs of media skills instruction. However, no book or journal article to date has presented a thoroughgoing model for integrating media skills instruction into the modern, empirical teaching process. This book provides such a model, as well as practical recommendations for the implementation of a media skills program in any school or school system.

We do not suggest that a program of media skills instruction is the sole function of the media center. Ongoing services and routines, including the evaluation and acquisition of instructional materials, assistance to students and staff in the use of those materials, media production services, reference services, bibliographic services, circulation control, and the myriad of other important media center functions must and should be continued. However, we do suggest that a systematic program of media skills instruction be developed gradually to supplant scheduled library periods, or programs of "library skills" unrelated to classroom units.

The instructional model presented here is not simply a theoretical construct. Rather, it is based on the authors' participation in the development and implementation of a media skills program in the 200 public schools of Montgomery

County, Maryland. Though not in any sense a faithful description of the Montgomery County approach, the book draws heavily on the practical experience provided by that program.

Rockville, Maryland
1976

PART I—MEDIA SKILLS INSTRUCTION

CHAPTER 1

TEACHING MEDIA SKILLS

INTRODUCTION

What Are Media Skills? The term "media skills" encompasses that group of student skills related to the gathering and utilization of information which in past educational usage was designated by such terms as "research skills," "study skills," and "library skills." Use of the newer term "media skills" properly recognizes our increasing reliance on information sources other than print and corresponds with the currency in education of the terms "media center" and "instructional media." At the same time, the term reflects the explosive proliferation of all kinds of media in our contemporary society.

The very vastness of the current information explosion implies the need, often left unrecognized by educators, for a cluster of media skills. In the face of millions of books, television programs, films, magazines, records, tapes, and film-strips presently available, one is confronted with the perplexing difficulty of locating specific information, selecting from among the numerous information sources available, using those sources, and comprehending their content regardless of medium. These problems are bewildering for the student, for he is constantly required by teachers and media specialists to locate and use information, but he has seldom been taught in any systematic way how to accomplish that task. The under-lying, unstated assumption of teachers has been that students somehow assimilate media skills somewhere along the way with only the most cursory formal instruction. Formal instruction has therefore been concentrated on the mechanics of library procedure and organization rather than on the essential skills involved in locating, selecting, using, and understanding instructional media. Students have been inundated with descriptive details of the card catalog and the Dewey Decimal System, but the actual location and use of needed information has been left largely to the imagination. At best, students may have received some brief instruction in media skills from the media specialist, and that instruction has often been unrelated or only tangentially related to classroom studies. Yet, modern educational tech-niques designed to individualize instruction rely more heavily than ever before on the student's ability to locate and utilize a wide variety of media materials.

Who Teaches Media Skills? The dilemma of media skills instruction, or rather the lack of media skills instruction, is that such instruction has not been clearly the responsibility of any one school staff member. Some school systems have established brief units, often neglected by teachers, relating to study or research skills. But in the absence of such units, the task of instructing an entire

11

student body in media and research skills often falls, by default, to a single media specialist.

In the past decade, media specialists have made remarkable strides in establishing themselves as full-fledged members of the school instructional staff. It is not so very long since the school library was regarded as a passive depository of printed information only roughly related to the mainstream of instruction, and the school librarian was the step-sister of the teaching staff. That antique notion has been superseded, largely through the professional efforts of school librarians, by the unified media concept, which identifies the media center as the very core of the school, housing all the media and materials of instruction and actively changing to reflect every innovation in the curriculum or instructional style of the school. The media specialist is not only the keeper of the media center and media collection, but an active participant in the instructional planning process, a supporting participant in everyday instruction, and the staff member charged with primary responsibility for teaching media skills. Such is the unified media philosophy articulated and promoted with considerable success by media specialists. But is it altogether practical?

Can the Media Specialist Do It Alone? Perhaps media specialists, in their understandable zeal to establish the unified media concept in the common educational wisdom, have somehow overstated the case. Is it really reasonable to expect one media specialist—and it still *is* usually only one, despite the American Library Association's staffing standards[1]—to be thoroughly familiar with all aspects of school curriculum, maintain a media collection consistent with that curriculum, participate in daily instructional planning, give instructional support in everyday teaching, and take full charge of an instructional program in media skills for all students?

Probably not. In fact, media specialists, in their literature, have long recognized the need for the assistance of teachers in media skills instruction and for relating media skills instruction to other classroom teaching. The assistance of teachers is vital since it is unreasonable to expect that a media specialist can single-handedly impart a large body of information to every student. Integrating media skills into ordinary classroom instruction is also essential, since it provides an immediate practical application for information that is often, in the students' eyes, arcane. What has been lacking in the past is an instructional model which successfully integrates media skills instruction with classroom instruction, and which suggests a systematic combination of the efforts of teachers and media specialists.

A PLAN FOR MEDIA SKILLS INSTRUCTION

Modern teaching is generally conceived as a cylical process involving a number of clearly defined components (see Figure 1). The process begins with the formulation of precise instructional objectives, derived from broad educational goals and specifying the content to be taught and the behavior to be elicited from students. Methods and learning activities are then developed, based on the intellectual level and learning style of students and on the nature of the subject matter to be taught. Instructional resources are selected, and teaching is implemented. Students are evaluated, using tests or other assessment measures that correspond exactly to the

Figure 1: General Teaching Model

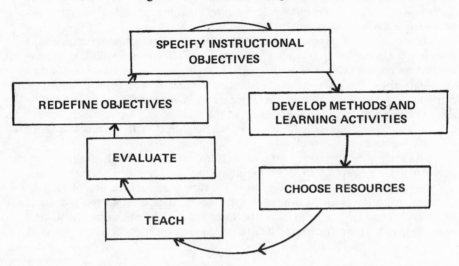

student behavior specified in the instructional objectives. On the basis of student performance, objectives may be redefined for future instruction, and the teaching cycle begins again.

If the teaching process is really so simple, why has the teaching of media skills been so fraught with difficulties? In a Spring 1972 article in *School Libraries*, Eleanor Ahlers suggests that several basic problems account for the difficulties. First, teachers still lack preparation in the use of instructional media and the role of the media center in teaching. Second, media specialists lack preparation in current educational theory and practice. Third, there is a lack of communication and information exchange between teachers and media specialists and a lack of time during the school day for joint planning.[2]

Admittedly, these are difficult problems, but they are probably not so difficult as often imagined. In formal professional preparation, teachers are increasingly receiving instruction in multi-media methods, and media specialists are taught the basics of educational theory and technique. Additionally, in-service training efforts in many school systems throughout the country have been designed specifically to fill gaps in the formal educational preparation of both teachers and media specialists regarding the use of instructional media and the function of the media center. As teachers and media specialists grow to understand their respective roles and functions, the communication problem vanishes, albeit slowly.

Lack of joint planning time is a less tractable problem. Often, however, it is not so much a genuine lack of time as it is a misunderstanding of exactly what is to be planned and how to plan it. Once a real understanding of the joint planning process is developed by both teacher and media specialist, "lack of time" becomes chimerical.

All of these impediments to teaching media skills cited by Ms. Ahlers and recognized by others are, in truth, expressions of a more subtle and general problem. Media specialists, in the past, have sought to "relate" media skills instruction to everyday classroom teaching rather than to integrate the two. Teachers, on the other hand, have been perfectly willing for media specialists to "relate" media skills to classroom studies but have not, typically, *integrated* media skills objectives, activities, and assessments into instruction.

The difference between the terms "relate" and "integrate" seems subtle at first, but the operational difference is enormous. *Relating* media skills to classroom instruction implies one set of instructional objectives and a separate set of media skills objectives, one set of instructional activities and a separate set of media skills activities, one set of instructional assessments and a separate set of media skills assessments, all more or less related but, at the same time, all very much separate. *Integrating* media skills *into* classroom instruction, on the other hand, implies only one set of instructional objectives, activities, and assessments.

An integrated approach to media skills instruction takes advantage of the strength and preparation of the teacher in instructional theory and methodology and the strength of the media specialist in the theory and application of instructional media. Instructional planning for media skills then emerges as a process of logically and equitably dividing labor between teacher and media specialist. An example may best illustrate how such an integrated process operates in practice.

AN EXAMPLE OF AN INTEGRATED APPROACH TO MEDIA SKILLS INSTRUCTION

School XYZ is an elementary school of traditional design in a middle-class suburban community. Students are divided into discrete K-6 classes and teaching follows the usual one-teacher-per-class model, though occasional team-teaching is encouraged and practiced. There is a media specialist at the school who has achieved considerable rapport with the teaching staff and has gained both administrative and parental support for media center programs. She has determined to undertake a systematic approach to teaching media skills and to integrate media skills instruction with daily classroom teaching. Here, for example, is how she integrated instruction in alphabetizing, use of indexes, and various media-production skills into a third-grade science unit on animal habitats.

Two third-grade teachers developed the following instructional objectives for their unit on animal habitats:

1. Students will observe animals in their natural environments and record observations.
2. Students will identify the behavioral attributes of animals in their natural environment from direct observation and from print and nonprint resources.
3. Students will identify similarities and differences in the behavior of animals in their natural environments from direct observation and from print and nonprint resources.
4. Students will identify the interrelationships of animals, plants, and other environmental conditions (e.g., climate, weather, physical topography, etc.) from direct observation and from print and nonprint resources.
5. Students will predict animal behavior in relation to environmental variables.

The activities planned for the accomplishment of these objectives included direct observation and recording of animal behavior under natural and controlled conditions. However, the teachers recognized the need for students to locate and use information about animal habitats in addition to their observations. Moreover, it was recognized that the students needed to assemble their recorded observations into some kind of culminating activity.

When the teachers consulted the media specialist after school concerning the availability of support materials on animal habitats, the media specialist examined the proposed unit objectives and suggested the following additions:

1. Students will use a simple book index to locate information on animal habitats.
2. Students will produce a slide set, a mural, or a series of transparencies based on their recorded observation of animal environments and on information derived from print and nonprint resources.

These two objectives were incorporated by the teachers into their instructional objectives for the unit, and the media specialist, in consultation with the teachers, developed a number of activities to accomplish the two objectives.

Class activities began with a nature walk to a nearby park, during which students observed local animals, their homes, eating habits, bodily adaptation to environment, and interaction with other living things. Observations were recorded and, upon returning to class, experiences were compared and listed on a composite chart. In ensuing discussion, students were encouraged to recognize not only the wealth of information they had been able to discover from simple observation, but also the information they had not been able to obtain, particularly regarding animals and habitats other than the local variety. Obviously, research was required, providing a perfect pre-planned opportunity for the media specialist to teach the use of simple indexes for locating needed information.

The media specialist recognized that alphabetizing skills were necessary if the students were to use an index in locating information on animal habitats. Although she had previously instructed students in alphabetizing in relation to a language arts unit that incorporated beginning dictionary skills, she developed an alphabetizing pre-test using materials related to animals and animal habitats. Using a sound effects record, she recorded a group of familiar animal sounds designed to be used in connection with the alphabetizing pre-test shown in Figure 2, page 16.

The alphabetizing pre-test was set up as a learning center within the media center, and the third graders came by classroom reading groups to the media center to take the pre-test. On the basis of their previous instruction in alphabetizing, most students had no difficulty in performing well. However, for those students who had difficulty, several games and activities were designated to strengthen alphabetizing skills.

Once students had been pre-tested on alphabetizing and as they were proceeding with classroom activities related to the observation, recording, and discussion of animal behavior, the media specialist developed a very brief expository lesson on book indexes and four simple learning centers based on resources related to animal habitats and incorporating indexes from those resources (see Figure 3 through Figure 6 beginning on page 17). The centers were designed specifically to answer questions arising from classroom discussion.

Figure 2: Alphabetizing Pre-Test

You have heard all of these sounds before. Turn on the tape recorder and listen to the sounds. Circle the name of the animal which makes the sound which you hear.

1. lions	wolves	dogs	coyotes
2. ducks	dogs	leopard	cat
3. dog	elephant	catbird	cat
4. duck	song bird	chicken	crow
5. lizards	birds	insects	frogs
6. sea lions	frogs	chimpanzee	toads
7. hyenas	elephants	tigers	lions
8. turkeys	chickens	flamingo	ducks
9. ducks	chickens	goats	turkeys
10. baby	sheep dog	burro	sheep

Stop the tape recorder and make sure that you have circled an animal for every number. Turn on the tape recorder and check your paper for the correct answers. When you have corrected your paper, put the names of the animals correctly circled in alphabetical order below.

1. _____ 6. _____
2. _____ 7. _____
3. _____ 8. _____
4. _____ 9. _____
5. _____ 10. _____

Turn on the tape recorder to check your paper for the correct alphabetical arrangement.

Figure 3: Endangered Species

This is the simplest center. It uses the book and index from the book, *Wildlife in Danger* by Ivah Green. There are three activity cards to be done in sequence. The pictures on the center are the same animals featured on the cards to be alphabetized in activity one. Pictures and names of the animals are included on the cards. Animals included are: eagle, coyote, flamingo, heron, Key deer, wolf, walrus, manatee, and grizzly bear. The instructor keeps the answers.

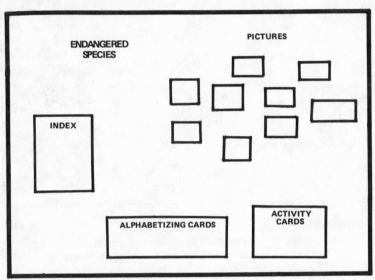

Activity Card One
  A.   Remove the alphabetizing cards from the pocket.
  B.   Look at the words and pictures on each card.
  C.   Put the cards in alphabetical order and write the words in that order on your paper.

Activity Card Two
  A.   Remove the alphabetizing cards from the pocket.
  B.   Using the index, find the names of the animals and write the page numbers on which information about that animal is found.

<u>animal</u>   <u>page</u>

Activity Card Three
  A.   Use the index to find the answer to these questions.
  B.   On your paper, write the word in the sentence that you used to look for that question in the index. Fill in the blanks in the question, and then answer the question.
       1.   Is there a picture of a walrus on page _____ ?
       2.   Is there a picture of a heath hen on page _____ ?
       3.   Is there a colored picture of an Eskimo Curlew on page _____ ?
       4.   Is there a colored picture of a Carolina Paroquet on page _____ ?

Figure 4: Horses

This center is based on the book and index, *The Story of Horses*, by D. E. Shuttlesworth. It has four activity cards to be done in sequence. There are nine pictures of horses on the center. The instructor keeps the answer cards.

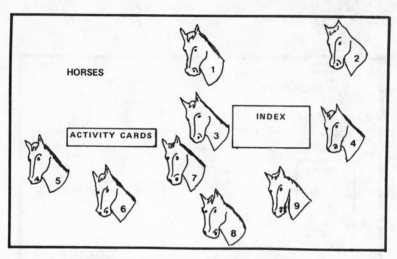

Activity Card One
- A. Look at the picture of each horse on the center.
    1. Quarter Horse
    2. Lipizzan
    3. Palomino
    4. Appaloosa
    5. Clydesdale
    6. Morgan Horse
    7. Pinto
    8. Shetland Pony
    9. Standardbred
- B. Put these in alphabetical order.

Activity Card Two
- A. Look up each of these horses' names in the index.
- B. Identify on your paper the page number where information about the horse may be found.

Activity Card Three
- A. Turn to the pages which the index shows will give information about each of the horses.
- B. Write the name of the place where these horses usually live.
- C. Write how each horse is used by man.

Activity Card Four
- A. Write which pages will give information on the following:
    1. ponies _____
    2. mules _____
    3. prehistoric horses _____
    4. breeds of horses _____
    5. wild horses _____
    6. jumping _____
    7. color of horses _____
    8. donkey _____
    9. bronco _____
    10. eyesight of horses _____

Figure 5: Animals

This center consists of four activities based on the book and index, *A Field Guide to Animal Tracks* by Olaus Murie. It includes the book, a tape of animal sounds, a box of 20 plastic animal replicas, and 15 pictures of animal tracks from the book with the animal name by each track. Label some incorrectly. The instructor has the answers.

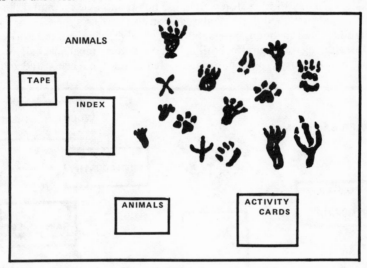

Activity Card One
- A. Identify the twenty plastic animals in the box using the picture dictionary.
- B. Arrange these animals in alphabetical order.
- C. Write the names of these animals in order on your paper.

Activity Card Two
- A. Choose ten animals from the container.
- B. Find the names of these animals in the index.
- C. Find and write the page numbers where information on these animals may be found.

Activity Card Three
- A. Play the tape of animal sounds.
- B. Identify each sound.
- C. Find the name of the animal which makes each sound in the index and give the page number where its tracks may be found.

Acitivity Card Four
- A. Look at each of the animal tracks on the center.
- B. Choose five animal tracks.
- C. Find the names of the animals in the index.
- D. Tell whether or not the track on the center is correct according to the book.

Figure 6: African Animals

This center is based on the books, *Africa's Animals* by Marvin Newman and Eliot Elisofon and *The Wildlife of Africa* by Jocelyn Arundel. It is a difficult center and involves four activities using *Africa's Animals*, which has no index, and *Wildlife of Africa*, which has an index.

There are 25 pictures of African animals with names mounted and laminated on clear plastic (or x-ray film), a stop watch, the books and index, a mural illustrating types of habitats included in the center, and answer cards.

Animals included: baboon, bongo, buffalo, cheetah, chimpanzee, crocodile, eland, elephant, gazelle, giraffe, gorilla, hippopotamus, impala, jackal, kudo, leopard, lion, monkey, oryx, ostrich, pangolin, rhinoceros, wildebeest, and zebra.

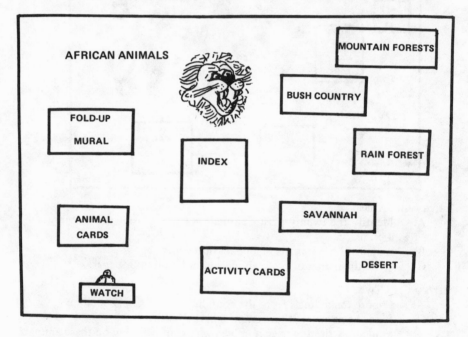

Activity Card One
  A. Remove the clear animal name cards from the pocket.
  B. Lay the cards on the table and put the animals' names in alphabetical order.
  C. Write the animal names in order on your paper.

Activity Card Two
  A. Choose 10 pictures.
  B. Find these animals' names in the index on the center.
  C. Write the page numbers on which information about these animals can be found.

(Figure 6 is continued on page 21.)

Figure 6 (cont'd)

Activity Card Three
   A.   Remove five animal cards (baboon, chimpanzee, etc.).
   B.   Using the stop watch, you are first to find the pages in *African Animals* (which has no index) on which information on the five animals may be found. Write the animal and page number and time it took to find the right page.
   C.   Next, find the same five animals and page numbers in the book *with* the index, using the stop watch. Write the name, page, and time.

Activity Card Four
   A.   Choose the 10 animal cards which you haven't used yet.
   B.   Find these animals in the index on the center. Using the page numbers found, look for the animal in the book.
   C.   Place the animals in the pockets which show where those animals live.
   D.   Remove the mural and unfold it.
   E.   After unfolding the mural, put the animal in its correct habitat:

Desert	Mountain Forest
Savannah	Rain Forest
Bush Country	

(The definition of the habitat is on the pocket.)

Meanwhile, as classroom activities continued, groups of students went to the media center to use the index centers and, once indexing skills had been mastered through use of the four centers, applied those skills to gathering information related to classroom activities. Based on the information gathered, the teachers identified with the students six specific habitats: swamps, deserts, mountains, prairies, forests, and foreign environments (specifically of Africa). Students were allowed to select one habitat around which their culminating activity would center, namely, the preparation of a series of slides, a mural, or a series of color lift transparencies on their chosen habitat. The resulting six groups of students gathered additional print and nonprint materials on the selected habitat. At the same time, the media specialist instructed the groups of students in media techniques necessary for the completion of the culminating activities which they had selected earlier (i.e., slide production techniques, preparation of transparencies, and murals).

AN INTEGRATED MODEL FOR
MEDIA SKILLS INSTRUCTION

The foregoing example suggests distinct differences between "relating" and "integrating" media skills into classroom instruction, as illustrated in Figures 7 and 8 (page 22). In the unintegrated or "related" model (Figure 7), teachers and media specialists respectively develop totally separate objectives, activities, and assessments, and though these may be verbally related by teacher and media specialist, they are not operationally interdependent. In the integrated model (Figure 8), as illustrated by the example, instructional objectives and media skills

Figure 7: Related Model of Media Skills Instruction

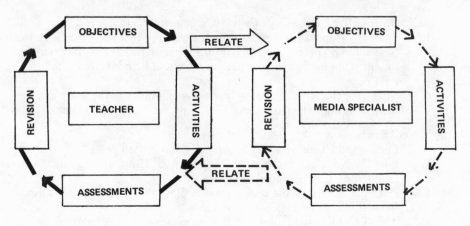

Figure 8: Integrated Model of Media Skills Instruction

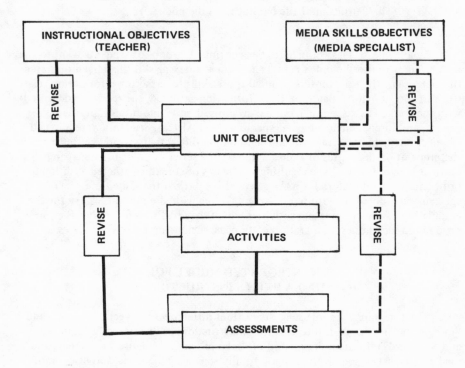

objectives may be separately formulated, owing to the subject expertise of teachers and the media skills expertise of media specialists. However, in planning a teaching unit, instructional objectives and media skills objectives are merged into one set of unit objectives. Thereafter, media skills activities derive their subject matter directly and perhaps exclusively from the unit of study, and classroom teaching activities depend in large part on media skills instruction. In fact, the distinction between instructional objectives, activities, and assessments on the one hand, and media skills objectives, activities, and assessments on the other become specious as the two are merged into a single instructional unit.

Succeeding chapters will further explore each component of this integrated model of media skills instruction and will provide practical suggestions for the planning and implementation of a school media skills program.

SUMMARY

Media skills are student skills related to the gathering and utilization of information. Instructional objectives, activities, and assessments for media skills are ideally integrated into classroom objectives, activities, and assessments, and the resulting instructional unit is taught jointly by teachers and media specialists. Since media skills objectives, activities, and assessments and classroom objectives, activities, and assessments are operationally interdependent in the recommended integrated instructional model, planning for media skills instruction becomes a simple process of equitably dividing labor between teacher and media specialist.

NOTES

[1] American Association of School Librarians, ALA, and Association for Educational Communications and Technology, *Media Programs: District and School* (Chicago, American Library Association, 1975).

[2] Eleanor E. Ahlers, "Instruction in Library Skills," *School Libraries*, Spring 1972, pp. 23-25.

BIBLIOGRAPHY

Ahlers, Eleanor E. "Instruction in Library Skills." *School Libraries* 21:3 (Spring 1972), pp. 23-25.

American Association of Elementary-Kindergarten-Nursery Educators. *Elementary School Media Program: An Approach to Individualizing Instruction.* Washington, D.C., National Education Association, n.d.

American Association of School Librarians and Association for Educational Communications and Technology. *Media Programs: District and School.* Chicago, American Library Association and Association for Educational Communications and Technology, 1974.

Davies, Ruth Ann. *The School Library Media Center: A Force for Educational Excellence.* New York, Bowker, 1974.

Gillespie, John T., and Spirt, Diana L. *Creating a School Media Program.* New York, Bowker, 1973.

Glogau, Lillian; Krause, Edmund; and Wexler, Miriam. *Developing a Successful Elementary School Media Center.* West Nyack, N.Y., Parker Publishing Co., 1972.

Nicholson, Margaret E. "The I.M.C." *School Libraries*, March 1964, pp. 39-43.

Prostano, Emanuel E., and Prostano, Joyce S. *The School Library Media Center.* 2nd ed. Littleton, Colo., Libraries Unlimited, 1977.

Rossoff, Martin. *The School Library and Educational Change.* Littleton, Colo., Libraries Unlimited, 1971.

Sullivan, Peggy. *Impact: The School Library and the Instructional Program.* Chicago, American Library Association, 1967.

CHAPTER 2

OBJECTIVES FOR MEDIA SKILLS

There are two kinds of educational objectives: general educational objectives (program objectives) and instructional objectives. The two have very different functions, and may be distinguished by how specifically they indicate exact and observable student behavior. Since both are essential to the successful implementation of a program of media skills instruction, both will be examined in some detail.

Program Objectives. Program objectives, or general educational objectives, are the broad, often abstract goals of educational systems or programs. While they may vary considerably in specificity, they are usually general philosophical statements that incorporate such language as "understand," "appreciate," and "value."

Though lately in bad repute owing to the movement toward behaviorally stated instructional objectives, general program objectives do serve the useful functions of relating educational values to the broad cultural values of society, and relating the general features of one educational program to another (e.g., the language arts program to the science program, the media program to the social studies program, etc.). It is this second function—that is, of relating various educational programs—that James Liesener identifies as the principal utility of program objectives for media services.[1]

In Liesener's view, media services, including media skills instruction, are valuable only in relation to the broader goals and objectives of the "embedding" educational institution. This value may be indirect, in the form of services to teachers, or direct, in the form of services (or instruction) to students, but the relative distribution of alternative media services must be directly related to the general objectives of the entire instructional program.

What, then, are the program objectives for media skills instruction, and how closely are they related to broad educational goals?

PROGRAM OBJECTIVES FOR
MEDIA SKILLS INSTRUCTION

The general objective for any program of media skills instruction is to produce a student who is an independent and effective user of media. The major categories of student skills included in this objective are:

1. The ability to *identify* and *locate* media materials, or specific contents of media materials, after a search.
2. The ability to *select* one media material over another, or one part of a material over another part, for some particular reason (matching, selecting, distinguishing).
3. The ability to *utilize*, *comprehend*, and *apply* information derived from media materials.
4. The ability to *produce*, *create*, or *present* media materials.

It is instructive to make a brief comparison between this general media skills objective and its four components and those general educational goals specified by Benjamin Bloom in his widely accepted taxonomy of educational objectives. Bloom divides educational goals into two categories: those related to the cognitive domain,[2] and those related to the affective domain.[3] Six major cognitive objectives are identified:

1. Knowledge (recall) of specifics (terminology, facts, ways and means, conventions, trends, sequences, classifications, criteria, universals, abstractions, principles, generalizations, theories, structures).
2. Comprehension, including translation, interpretation, extrapolation.
3. Application of knowledge.
4. Analysis of elements, relationships, and organizational principles.
5. Synthesis of information, including production of a plan, unique communication, or set of derived abstract relations.
6. Evaluation of materials and methods, including judgments based on internal evidence and external criteria.

Media skills program objectives are clearly related to each of these cognitive objectives. They constitute an area of knowledge in themselves, and also are requisite to learning in nearly every other field of knowledge. Similarly, comprehension, application of knowledge, analysis of elements, synthesis of information, and evaluation of materials and methods are not only legitimate general objectives for media skills instruction, but the attainment of these objectives in media skills is necessary for the attainment of the same objectives in other disciplines.

There are, in Bloom's taxonomy, five major objectives in the affective domain:

1. Receiving (attending), including awareness, willingness to receive, and controlled or selected attention.
2. Responding, including acquiescence in responding, willingness to respond, and satisfaction in response.
3. Valuing.
4. Organization of values and value systems.
5. Characterization by a value or value complex.

Again, as in the cognitive domain, media skills objectives are closely related to general affective objectives. Receiving (attending to) information depends upon skill in identifying, locating, and using media; responding requires the ability to produce print and nonprint media; and value formation in every area of knowledge requires the ability to locate and evaluate sources of information.

Comparing media skills program objectives with other systems of classifying educational goals yields similar results. Without further belaboring the point, it is clear that media skills are an integral part of many major educational goals and are essential to the accomplishment of others. But, as indicated in Chapter 1, it is at the level of instructional objectives, activities, and assessments, that the genuine integration of media skills instruction into other classroom teaching occurs.

INSTRUCTIONAL OBJECTIVES FOR MEDIA SKILLS

Although program objectives are valuable as general statements of educational purpose, their vagueness makes them less useful in specific instructional units and lessons. "Students will learn to appreciate good literature" may be a perfectly legitimate program objective for media skills. But what learning activities does it suggest? How will it be observed in students? How will it be tested? Will students tell the teacher that they appreciate good literature, or will they be observed to devour it voraciously? In fact, the phrase "learn to appreciate good literature" does not answer any of these questions, and yet they must all be answered in planning units and lessons. Another kind of objective is obviously required—one that exactly specifies an observable student behavior. Once an observable behavior is specified, the process of designing learning activities that will produce the desired behavior, and tests or other assessments that will measure that behavior, becomes straightforward. For example, a "behavioral" or "instructional" objective related to the appreciation of good literature might read as follows: "Students will read *Island of the Blue Dolphin* and identify the theme of the book in a short paragraph." This objective specifies observable behavior, indicates a learning activity, and suggests an assessment (the accuracy of the theme summary). It is not as grandiose as "appreciating good literature," but it is certainly more instructionally manageable.

In their review of the literature on educational objectives, Kibler, Cegala, Barker, and Miles identify a number of other compelling reasons for the exact indication of student behavior in instructional objectives, and many of these reasons are particularly important in the development of instructional objectives for media skills.[4]

First, the use of behaviorally stated instructional objectives is a useful guide to teacher and media specialist accountability. Though accountability is sometimes regarded as vaguely threatening, it is only reasonable to expect some positive behavioral change in students in exchange for the vast amounts of money expended on media staff, materials, and equipment, and such behavioral change is not likely to be observed unless it is clearly specified. Moreover, the statement of media skills objectives in behavioral terms allows teachers and media specialists to communicate to each other *exactly* what is to be taught, to arrange logical sequences of instructional units, and to design learning activities that produce student behaviors satisfying both classroom instructional objectives and media skills objectives. It is obviously easier for teachers, media specialists, *and* students to deal with clear objectives ("students will use a simple book index to locate information on animal habitats") than vague statements ("students will understand how to use the library"). The former provide a guide to teachers and media specialists concerning what is to be taught, how to teach it, and how to assess student performance. The latter give no such indication.

A SEQUENCE OF MEDIA SKILLS OBJECTIVES

Before providing a recommended sequence of instructional objectives for media skills, it is necessary to recognize two kinds of instructional objectives. First, there are general instructional objectives, typically found in curriculum guides, which are both subject-specific and behaviorally stated. Even more specific, however, are performance objectives, which are lesson objectives, stating the exact student behaviors to be elicited in a lesson or series of lessons.

Though this distinction between general instructional objectives and performance objectives is not consistently made in the literature of education, it is particularly useful. In Chapter 1, it was stated that classroom instructional objectives and media skills objectives might be separately formulated by teachers and media specialists, owing to the subject expertise of teachers and the media skills expertise of media specialists. It is at the level of lesson planning—the formulation of performance objectives—that media skills objectives and classroom instructional objectives are merged into a single unit of instruction.

To illustrate further this important distinction, let us return briefly to the example cited in Chapter 1. In planning the unit on animal habitats, the media specialist has suggested the inclusion of two performance objectives in the unit:

1. Students will use a simple book index to locate information on animal habitats.
2. Students will produce a slide set, a mural, or a series of transparencies based on their recorded observation of animal environments.

These objectives were carefully planned with teachers and were stated precisely in terms of the subject matter of the instructional unit. However, the more general instructional objectives for media skills—e.g., "students will use a simple book index," "students will produce slides," "students will produce transparencies," etc.—need not have been jointly planned. In fact, owing to the scarcity of joint planning time, it is highly desirable for the media specialist to formulate independently a complete sequence of media skills objectives so that when planning with teachers does occur, it can be a simple and efficient process of choosing those media skills objectives which best fit a given set of classroom instructional objectives.

Obviously, it is necessary for teachers to be familiar with the entire sequence of media skills objectives just as it is necessary for the media specialist to be familiar with the entire sequence of classroom instructional objectives. Joint planning sessions, then, involve the formulation of performance objectives for the unit of study which incorporate both classroom instructional objectives and media skills objectives. The two major planning guides are curriculum guides and a written sequence of media skills objectives.

The sequence of media skills objectives presented in Figures 9 through 12 (beginning on page 30) is not to be regarded as inviolable. Local variations in curriculum, student population, media collections and equipment, and so forth will suggest numerous additions, deletions, and grade level changes. The sequence is presented as a sample based on the authors' experience in school media skills instruction and in developing and implementing a media skills program in a large county school system. It is intended as a guide to the formulation of a sequence of objectives that suit local needs. It is *not* intended as an iron-bound document that proscribes the introduction of a particular skill at a level earlier than the suggested level, or the reinforcement of particular skill at a later level.

The instructional objectives in the sample sequence are grouped into the four major categories of student skills earlier identified as the components of the program objective "to produce a student who is an independent and effective user of media":

1. The ability to *identify* and *locate* media materials, or specific contents of media materials, after a search.
2. The ability to *select* one media material over another, or one part of a material over another part, for some particular reason.
3. The ability to *utilize*, *comprehend*, and *apply* information derived from media materials.
4. The ability to *produce*, *create*, or *present* media materials.

Within each category, objectives are subgrouped by grade levels, with simple skills presented at early levels and more complex variations of the same skill presented at subsequent levels. Conversely, objectives at higher levels, depend upon student attainment of objectives at lower levels, both within the same category and in the other three categories. For example, an objective in the "selection" category which is recommended for introduction in grade four is: "the student will select and distinguish among volumes of an encyclopedia which is arranged alphabetically to find information on a given topic." This objective depends upon alphabetizing objectives introduced at levels K-4 in the "utilization, comprehension, application" category. It also depends upon objectives in other categories at the *same* level; for example, upon the objective at level 4 in the "identification, location" category "students will identify and locate encyclopedias."

WRITING PERFORMANCE OBJECTIVES

The objectives in the sample sequence (beginning on page 30) fulfill the most important condition for instructional objectives—that is, that they describe *observable* student behavior. Terms such as "operate," "identify," "locate," and "use" describe observable behavior, whereas the terms "understand" and "appreciate" do not. However, in writing performance objectives for particular lessons in media skills, two other conditions should be met if the objectives are to conform to the widely accepted criteria proposed by Robert Mager:[5]

1. The objective must specify the *conditions* under which the student will achieve the objective; i.e., materials, equipment, time limits, etc.
2. The objective must specify the *criterion* for successful completion of the objective (e.g., the student will get 50 percent correct). If no criterion is specified, it is assumed that students must complete the entire objective with total accuracy.

Figure 9: A Sequence of Media Skills Objectives

IDENTIFICATION AND LOCATION

The student will:

K-1	2	3	3 (cont'd)
Identify and locate:	Identify:	Identify and locate:	Locate material and information using:
a. picture or easy materials	a. the title of a print or non-print item	a. the card catalog	a. a title page
b. picture dictionaries	b. the author of a print or nonprint item	b. book catalogs	b. a table of contents
c. records	c. the illustrator of a print or nonprint item	c. the vertical file	c. a map list
d. record players	d. publisher of a print or nonprint item	d. periodicals	d. an illustration list
e. cassettes	e. the place of publication of a print or nonprint item	e. newspapers	e. a time table
f. cassette tape recorders	f. the copyright date or date of publication of a print or nonprint item	f. dictionaries	f. a simple map
g. filmstrips		g. the telephone directory	g. an index
h. filmstrip previewers		h. transparencies	Identify and locate in a newspaper:
i. filmloops	Identify and locate:	i. overhead projectors	a. sections of the paper
j. filmloop projectors	a. the fiction collection	j. micro-projectors	b. the index of the paper
k. listening station and ear phones	b. the non-fiction collection	k. maps and globes	
l. language master cards	c. slides	Identify and locate in a print item:	
m. language master	d. slide previewers	a. the title page	
n. kits (audio-visual)	e. opaque projectors	b. the table of contents	
o. sound filmstrip previewer		c. an illustration list	
p. realia		d. a map list	
Locate specific picture or easy book materials using the author's last name (if so arranged)		e. a time table	
		f. an index	
Identify in a book:		Locate a specific item of information in:	
a. the front of the print item		a. a title page	
b. the back of the print item		b. a table of contents	
c. the spine of the print item		c. an illustration list	
		d. a map list	
		e. a time table	
		f. an index	

Figure 9 (cont'd)

IDENTIFICATION AND LOCATION

The student will:

4	5	6	7-8
Identify and locate: a. encyclopedias b. tapes (reel) c. tape recorders (reel to reel) d. pamphlets, clippings, etc. in the vertical file e. dry mount press Locate specific sources in the card catalog by author, title, or subject Locate a specific resource in the media center using the call number of the print or nonprint item given on a catalog card. Identify and locate materials using the *Dewey Decimal System of Classification.* Locate specific information about an item on the catalog card. Identify and locate in a print item: a. guide words b. a glossary	Identify and locate: a. indexes b. the index or guide to children's periodicals c. almanacs d. atlases e. special dictionaries f. slide projectors g. films (8mm and 16mm) h. 8mm and 16mm film projectors Identify and locate in a print item: a. an appendix b. cross references	Identify and locate: a. a camera (visual maker, etc.) b. video tapes c. video tape recorders d. a thesaurus e. specific reference materials	Identify and locate: a. microforms b. microform viewers c. copying machines d. bibliographies e. *Reader's Guide to Periodical Literature.*

Figure 10: A Sequence of Media Skills Objectives

SELECTION

The student will:

K-1	2	3
Select: a. materials which are of personal interest b. a picture dictionary in order to match words with pictures c. an audio playing device for listening d. a visual projection device for examining pictures, etc. e. a listening station or earphones to individualize a listening experience f. realia Select and match: a. a record with a record player to listen to recorded sounds b. a cassette with a cassette tape recorder to play or record sounds c. a filmstrip with a filmstrip previewer to see a visual image d. a filmloop with a filmloop projector to view a moving visual image e. a language master card with a language master machine f. an audio-visual kit with a sound/filmstrip previewer or projector	Select: a. print and nonprint materials appropriate to ability level b. fiction materials for an account of imaginary happenings c. non-fiction materials for an account of factual or "real" information and occurrences Select and match: a. a slide with a slide previewer to look at visual images b. an item to be enlarged with an opaque projector	Select: a. periodicals and newspapers for current information b. a dictionary to find the meaning of a word c. the vertical file for pamphlet information d. a telephone directory to find correct numbers to be dialed Select and match: a. a filmstrip with a filmstrip projector for showing visuals b. a transparency with an overhead projector c. a slide with a microprojector Distinguish among various parts of a print item and select the part appropriate to locating specific information (parts include the title page, table of contents, illustration list, map list, index, etc, corresponding with designated ability level).

Figure 10 (cont'd)

SELECTION

The student will:

4	5	6	7-8
Select: a. resources using the card catalog and/or book catalog, given a specific subject, author, or title b. an encyclopedia to find information on a given subject c. a dictionary to find correct pronunciations of words, word derivations, parts of speech, multiple word meanings, and syllabication Select and match: a. a reel tape with a reel-to-reel tape recorder to play or record audio information b. material sources with a dry mount press for mounting visual information Select and distinguish: a. between a dictionary and an encyclopedia b. among volumes of an encyclopedia which is arranged alphabetically to find information on a given topic	Select and match: a. an 8mm or 16mm film with an 8mm or 16mm film projector to show moving pictures b. slides with a slide projector to show a series of visuals Select: a. an index to children's periodicals for current information on a given topic b. the appropriate index to find information on a given topic c. the appropriate sources and necessary instructional equipment given specific topics (geographical, biographical, quick factual, etc.)	Select a camera to record a visual image Distinguish between types of visual materials (posters, filmstrips, slides, etc.) and select appropriate items based on advantages and disadvantages of each type Select and match a videotape with a videotape recorder	Select: a. a reference source based on knowledge of its purpose b. material based on specific criteria (authority, date, relevance, usefulness, appropriateness, and accuracy) Select and match a microform with a microform viewer

The student will:

Figure 11: A Sequence of Media Skills Objectives

COMPREHENSION, UTILIZATION, AND APPLICATION

K-1	2	3
Alphabetize by the first letter in a word or first letter in an author's last name	Alphabetize to the second letter of a word or an author's last name	Alphabetize to the third letter of a word or an author's last name
Operate:	Operate:	Find words in a dictionary
a. a record player	a. an opaque projector	Operate:
b. a cassette tape recorder	b. a slide previewer	a. an overhead projector
c. a listening station	Identify and trace:	b. a filmstrip projector
d. a filmstrip previewer	a. the development of a	c. a micro-projector
e. an 8mm filmloop projector	character (motivation)	Use:
f. a language master machine	b. the development of a plot	a. a telephone directory
g. a sound/filmstrip previewer	c. the setting of a story	b. sections of a news-paper and its indexes to locate specific infor-mation for a definite purpose
Identify and describe:	Identify:	
a. a written sequence of events	a. fantasy, unreality, impossibility, and incongruity in a resource	Predict:
b. a pictorial sequence of events	b. a fact, truth, reality, or possibility in a resource	a. actions of a character in a given situation
c. an audio sequence of events	Distinguish between fact and fiction	b. consequences of actions and events in a narrative
d. the main idea in diverse media materials	Predict the outcome of a narrative	Find directions on simple maps and globes
e. visual images using line, color, and shape		Interpret:
Use a picture dictionary		a. simple maps and globes
Find specific information:		b. simple graphs and charts
a. using picture clues in decoding		
b. using visuals (pictures, charts, filmstrips, etc.)		
c. listening to audio materials		

Figure 11 (cont'd)

COMPREHENSION, UTILIZATION, AND APPLICATION

The student will:

4	4 (cont'd)	5	5 (cont'd)

Alphabetize to the end of words and to the end of the author's last name
Alphabetize titles
Distinguish between word-by-word and letter-by-letter alphabetizing
Arrange materials using a specific system such as the *Dewey Decimal System of Classification*
Operate:
  a. a reel-to-reel tape recorder
  b. a dry mount press
State the purpose of basic information on catalog cards
Find specific information in materials using:
  a. guide words
  b. headings and sub-headings
  c. key words and phrases
  d. topic sentences
Identify and describe:
  a. the theme of a narrative (or main issue)
  b. the point of view of a narrative (or mood or tone)
  c. form or genre
	Skim materials to find a word, name, date, phrase, sentence, idea, or answer to a question
	Paraphrase simple information
	Use:
	  a. a map key to obtain information
	  b. a map scale to compute distance
	  c. a glossary to find the meaning for a word
	  d. a dictionary to find the meaning, part of speech, derivation, syllabication, and pronunciation of a word
	  e. an encyclopedia to locate information or solve a problem
		Use an appendix to locate material and information
		Operate:
		  a. an 8mm or 16mm film projector
		  b. a slide projector
		Identify alternate topics using cross references
		Use:
		  a. almanacs
		  b. atlases
		  c. gazetteers
		  d. simple guides to children's periodicals
		  e. special dictionaries (biographical, geographical, subject-oriented)
		Distinguish:
		  a. between main ideas and subordinate ideas
		  b. between a paraphrase, a summary, and use of direct quotations
		Prepare:
		  a. a simple outline
		  b. notes using a simple organizational pattern
		Summarize simple information found in resources
		Generalize information found in resources
			Interpret information found in resources (graphs, cartoons, map symbols, etc.)
			Compare:
			  a. ideas, facts, and visual images found in one resource for similarity, identity, difference, and contradiction
			  b. symbols and figures in maps
			Define a problem for research

(Figure 11 is continued on page 36.)

The student will:

Figure 11 (cont'd)

COMPREHENSION, UTILIZATION, AND APPLICATION

6	7-8	7-8 (cont'd)
Use: a. a thesaurus b. the index of special reference tools related to specific subject areas Operate: a. a simple camera b. a videotape recorder Skim to find material relevant to a topic Identify an opinion in a reference work (unsubstantiated statements) Support: a. a main idea using facts found in a specified reference source b. research on a problem or question using specified resource materials Organize information around a clearly defined topic Compare: a. figures in graphs to draw conclusions, make inferences, and make generalizations b. facts, ideas, visual images from more than one source Summarize information on a given topic from more than one source Draw conclusions on a given topic (inferences) from more than one source	Operate: a. a copy machine b. a microform viewer Identify: a. elements of a plot b. the author's style c. value judgments, premises, assumptions, hypotheses, evidence, arguments, and conclusions in a resource Plan a method of solving a problem using reference sources Use: a. a bibliography as an aid in locating information b. footnotes, marginal notes, and use of italics to discover author intent or emphasis c. footnotes to document information from resources d. all parts of a resource (table of contents, preface, etc.) as an aid in research e. subject-oriented resources to find specific information f. *Reader's Guide to Periodical Literature* g. more than one source to gather information	Prepare: a. notes in a specified form in presenting a report, giving credit when material is quoted b. a bibliography which follows a specified manual of style Recognize propaganda techniques in given resources Infer facts and ideas from a reading, map, graph, chart, cartoon, or other resource Predict trends, tendencies, or conditions presented in resources

Figure 12: A Sequence of Media Skills Objectives

PRODUCTION

The student will:

K-1	2	3
Translate oral or written directions from a resource into a product or action Record information on a cassette tape recorder Use color (hue, value, and intensity), line, and shape to produce a picture based on ideas in a story or reading Compose a title for a story, picture, chart, etc. Based on information from resources, compose a story which has a beginning, middle, and end	Illustrate a story or reading, by making a series of pictures, clay figures, creative movements Use a chosen method involving lines, shapes, colors, and textures to express ideas, feelings, or experiences obtained from a resource	Make: a. a simple map b. a simple chart c. a simple graph Prepare: a. a handmade transparency b. a color-life transparency c. a handmade slide d. a handmade filmstrip

(Figure 12 is continued on page 38.)

Figure 12 (cont'd)

PRODUCTION

The student will:

4	5	6	7-8
Mount a picture using a dry mount press (mount and laminate, etc.) Write and construct a model book which includes all specific parts of a book Use: a. lines, colors, shapes, and textures to create symbols b. sounds to create audio messages Produce media from appropriately chosen materials without teacher direction	Prepare: a. a reel-to-reel tape recording b. a slide c. a handmade film (16mm) Reproduce, with some degree of accuracy: a. what has been observed b. what has been heard Write a report using one chosen medium	Prepare: a. a filmstrip b. a film (filmloop) c. a videotape d. a slide presentation e. an audio-visual presentation Produce a media presentation that: a. expresses a mood or feeling b. contains specific subject matter c. has an identifiable theme or main issue d. shows sequential development of a character, theme, or main issue e. has a definite point of view	Prepare: a. a machine-made transparency b. a multi-media presentation c. a detailed report using audio-visual materials and equipment

Perhaps an example will best illustrate these conditions in the writing of performance objectives for media skills. One of the instructional objectives suggested in the sample sequence for introduction at level 2 is "the student will distinguish between fact and fiction." This instructional objective is part of the larger program objective "the student will utilize, comprehend, and apply information derived from media materials" (see Figure 11, page 34).

A media specialist had introduced the instructional objective "the student will distinguish between fact and fiction" to students in grade 2. However, he decided in planning with a sixth-grade teacher for an instructional unit on ancient Greece to reinforce that skill in grade six, and wrote the following performance objective for inclusion in that unit: "Given books on Greek mythology, non-fiction books on ancient Greece, and fiction books on ancient Greece, the student will identify those books which are factual and those which are fiction with 100 percent accuracy."

Notice the difference between the various levels of objectives in this example:

Program Objective:
> The student will utilize, comprehend, and apply information derived from media materials.

Instructional Objective:
> The student will distinguish between fact and fiction.

Performance Objective:
> Given books on Greek mythology, non-fiction books on ancient Greece, and fiction books on ancient Greece, the student will identify those books which are factual and those which are fiction with 100 percent accuracy.

The program objective indicates broad categories of behavior ("utilize," "comprehend," "apply"), but not behavior that is directly observable or related to a particular, specified action. The instructional objective is more specific with regard to observable behavior ("distinguish"), but it does not indicate the specific form of the behavior, its conditions, or any criterion of acceptable performance. The performance objective indicates a specifically observable behavior ("identify"), a condition of performance ("Given books on Greek mythology, non-fiction books on ancient Greece and fiction books on ancient Greece") and a criterion of acceptable performance ("100% accuracy"), though this criterion of acceptable performance is frequently omitted if complete accuracy is required.

SUMMARY

There are two kinds of educational objectives: general educational objectives (program objectives) and instructional objectives. The category "instructional objectives" may be further subdivided into general instructional objectives and performance objectives.

Program objectives for media skills are necessary in order to relate media instruction to the broad educational objectives of the "embedding" institution.

A written sequence of instructional objectives is desirable for use in communicating to teachers the substance of media skills instruction and in the joint planning of such instruction by teachers and media specialists.

Finally, the design of precise performance objectives for media skills, keyed directly to classroom instructional units and specifying observable student behavior, conditions of performance, and performance criteria, allows the integration of classroom instructional objectives and media skills objectives into a single unit of instruction.

NOTES

[1] James W. Liesener, *A Systematic Process for Planning and Communicating Media Programs* (Chicago, American Library Association, 1975).

[2] Benjamin S. Bloom, ed., *Taxonomy of Educational Objectives: The Classification of Educational Goals; Handbook I, Cognitive Domain* (New York, David McKay, 1956).

[3] David R. Krathwohl, *et al.*, *Taxonomy of Educational Objectives: The Classification of Educational Goals; Handbook II, Affective Domain* (New York, David McKay, 1964).

[4] R. J. Kibler, *et al.*, *Objectives for Instruction and Evaluation* (Boston, Allyn and Bacon, 1974).

[5] R. F. Mager, *Preparing Instructional Objectives* (Palo Alto, Calif., Fearon, 1962).

BIBLIOGRAPHY

Bloom, Benjamin S., ed., *et al. Taxonomy of Educational Objectives—the Classification of Educational Goals, Handbook I: Cognitive Domain.* New York, David McKay, 1956.

Burns, Richard W. *New Approaches to Behavioral Objectives.* Dubuque, Iowa, W. C. Brown, 1972.

Deprospo, Ernest R., and Liesener, James W. "Media Program Evaluation: A Working Framework." *School Media Quarterly* 3:4 (Summer 1975), pp. 289-301.

Kibler, Robert J., *et al. Objectives for Instruction and Evaluation.* Boston, Allyn and Bacon, 1974.

Krathwohl, D. R., Bloom, B. S.; and Masia, B. B. *Taxonomy of Educational Objectives: The Classification of Educational Goals, Handbook II: Affective Domain.* New York, David McKay, 1964.

Liesener, James W., and Levitan, Karen M. *A Process for Planning School Media Programs: Defining Service Outputs, Determining Resource and Operational Requirements, and Estimating Program Costs.* College Park, Md., College of Library and Information Services, University of Maryland, 1972.

Mager, Robert F. *Goal Analysis.* Palo Alto, Calif., Fearon, 1972.

Mager, Robert F. *Preparing Instructional Objectives.* Palo Alto, Calif., Fearon, 1962.

Popham, W. J., ed. *Instructional Objectives: An Analysis of Emerging Issues.* Chicago, Rand McNally, 1969.

Rothstein, H. M. "Humanistic Approach to Behavioral Objectives." *English Journal* 60 (September 1971), pp. 760-762.

Walbesser, H. H. *Constructing Behavioral Objectives.* College Park, Md., Bureau of Educational Research, University of Maryland, 1966.

Williams, William W. *Establishing and Evaluating Instructional Objectives.* New York, W. W. Norton Co., Inc., 1970.

CHAPTER 3

MEDIA SKILLS INSTRUCTION

The joint formulation of performance objectives for media skills by teachers and media specialists is certainly the first step in a planned program of media skills instruction, but it is by no means the only consideration in such a program. Once media skills objectives have been developed and integrated into the instructional objectives for a classroom unit, a method of instruction must be chosen—a method that will accomplish the stated objectives and that is consistent with all the variables in a teaching environment.

Since many different methods of instruction may be employed to accomplish a given objective, we will first examine a variety of instructional methods, and then suggest the variables to be considered in chosing an appropriate method.

INSTRUCTIONAL METHODS

Teaching techniques have been dealt with extensively elsewhere, and it is not our purpose to review in detail the literature of instructional methods. However, it may be useful to describe briefly the major techniques and give an example of each in relation to media skills instruction.

Lecture. A lecture is the expository description of facts, theories, generalizations, terms, or processes by the teacher to a student or group of students. It is perhaps the most common and, given attentive students, the most efficient means of instruction, since it needs no materials, resources, or instructional aids other than teacher and students.

> Example: The media specialist lectures third grade students on the use of a simple book index to locate information for a classroom unit on animal habitats.

Discussion. In the discussion method, the teacher introduces a concept or topic and encourages free exchange of ideas either among students or between students and teacher. Discussions may be expository and carefully guided by the teacher, or heuristic and free-wheeling.

> Example: In connection with a classroom unit on the family, the media specialist asks second graders to read *Horton Hatches an Egg*, *Make Way for Ducklings*, and *Are You My Mother?* and discusses with them the various characteristics of mothers in each story.

Demonstration. Demonstration techniques require that the teacher show or simulate for students an object, event, procedure, or process. Though often wrongly associated only with scientific laboratory experiments, demonstration is in fact a common classroom method; it may be seen in examples ranging from simple demonstrations (e.g., showing young children how to hold a pencil properly) to complex simulations (e.g., simulating volcanic action with a plaster-of-Paris volcano and potassium dichromate).

> Example: The media specialist demonstrates to third grade students the proper method of preparing color-lift transparencies so that

they may use the technique in the culminating activity of their classroom unit on animal habitats.

Drill, Practice, Recitation. Drill, practice, and recitation may be used as a method of instruction or as a follow-up to some other method of instruction. The objective of the technique is, through repetition, to produce an automatic recall or response.

Example: The media specialist drills students in alphabetizing with a set of word cards. The words on the cards are vocabulary words from a language arts unit.

Field Trip. Field trips are effective either as a follow-up to classroom instruction, or as a form of initial instruction to be followed up in the classroom.

Example: In connection with a classroom unit on communication, and media center instruction on location and use of newspapers for obtaining current information, the media specialist and third grade teacher take students on a field trip to the local newspaper.

Role-playing. Role-playing is simply a short dramatization in which students assume designated roles in relation to a specified problem or topic. The technique is frequently used as a secondary method to provide a concrete example of some behavior pattern for classroom discussion, but it may on occasion be the primary means of instruction, as in the following example.

Example: After telling kindergarten students the story of *Three Billy Goats Gruff*, the media specialist asks students to act out the story in proper order as a lesson in primary sequencing skills.

Games. Instructional games usually present the student with a problem or situation requiring solution according to specified rules. The solution requires some particular skill which the student must master either before or during the game.

Example: Fourth grade students play a relay race using the card catalog and 3x5-inch cards on which the names of particular explorers are written. Two teams are involved, and students, one at a time from each team, examine the 3x5-inch cards, and walk quickly to the appropriate card catalog drawer in which information on the explorer may be found. After verification by the media specialist, students return to their teams and the relay continues.

Audiovisual Instruction. Audiovisual instruction is not really a separate method, since films, filmstrips, tapes, and so forth are in fact lectures, demonstrations, discussions, or simulated "field trips" in audiovisual form. In addition, audiovisual instructional materials are seldom used alone as a primary teaching method, but rather as a part of, follow-up to, or introduction to some other method.

Example: Fourth grade students watch a film on maps and globes as an introduction to the media specialist's lesson on finding directions in printed maps.

Reading. Assigned reading is such a common instructional method that it is often neglected in listings of teaching techniques. However, reading remains one of the primary methods of transmitting information to students.

Example: The media specialist asks groups of students to read selections from the *Encyclopedia Brown* series and solve the "mysteries" as part of an advanced second grade language arts unit on inference and prediction in reading.

Individual or Group Study: Projects. The assignment of individual or group projects is a method that relies heavily on the student's ability to do independent or guided research; it is frequently used in conjunction with other methods in an instructional unit.

Example: As part of a fifth-grade geography unit, students were asked to select a state in the United States, plan an imaginary trip to that state, and prepare a booklet which included travel routes, points of historical interest, food, lodging, etc. In connection with the project, the media specialist gave lessons on media skills necessary for its completion (e.g., map skills, use of indexes, use of the card catalog to locate specific sources, etc.).

Programmed Instruction. Programmed instruction utilizes a series of sequential, written instructions for students, which must be answered or performed correctly in order for the student to complete the activity or attain a specific performance level. Feedback and reinforcement is provided for the student at each step in the programmed sequence, and frequently "branching" instructions allow students who are progressing easily to skip certain steps, or require students who are having difficulty to perform additional steps.

A kind of programmed instruction commonly used in recent years for media skills instruction is the **learning center**, which is simply a unit of programmed instruction confined to a particular physical area of the classroom or media center for use by individual students or groups of students. Such centers may be used as a primary method of instruction, or as an introduction to other instruction, or as a reinforcement technique. They may be primarily diagnostic (pre-test or post-test), or primarily instructional. If instructional, they may be subject-oriented centers that incorporate both subject matter from classroom and media skills instruction, or they may be designed only to teach a particular media skill without reference to other subject matter. Since it is the contention of this book that media skills instruction must be carefully integrated into classroom teaching, most of the learning centers illustrated herein are either diagnostic or subject-oriented.

Example: Extensive examples of media skills learning centers have been provided in Chapter 1. Figure 2 (page 16) is a diagnostic center, and Figures 3 through 6 (beginning on page 17) are instructional centers of the subject-oriented variety.

Obviously, each of the methods may be approached either deductively (the "expository" approach)—that is, by a statement or demonstration of the principle to be taught followed by examples and discussion of that principle; or inductively (the "inquiry" approach)—that is, by an examination of examples and experiences from which a principle is derived. These approaches have been thoroughly described elsewhere.[1]

INSTRUCTIONAL VARIABLES

In choosing methods of instruction for media skills, it is necessary to consider not only the inherent advantages of a particular technique, but also a number of important variables in the school environment. These may be divided into six general categories, which include variables related to:

1. the community and student body
2. the school facilities
3. school organization and scheduling
4. the school instructional staff
5. the curriculum
6. instructional methods and approaches

Each of these categories of variables poses important questions that must be answered as teachers and media specialists plan media skills instruction:

Community and Student Body

What is the physical make-up of the community?

What is the socioeconomic status of the community?

What broad cultural values and interests are held by community members?

How active are community members in civic and educational functions?

What are the means of communication between the school and community?

What are some of the community resources?

What are the major interests of students?

What are student abilities and achievement levels?

How do student achievement levels differ from those in other schools in the county or system and in the nation?

What are student social and intellectual strengths and weaknesses?

School Facilities

What is the physical configuration of the school?

Are classrooms totally discrete, totally open, or some combination of the two?

Is there a media center?

Are there resource centers?

An auditorium?

A gym?

An all-purpose room?

Instructional Staff

How many teachers are there?
Is there a full-time media specialist?
Media and instructional paraprofessionals?
What is the professional training of the instructional staff?
What are the instructional philosophies of teachers?

School Organization and Scheduling

How is the school organized?
Into individual classes?
Team-taught class groups?
Levels?
Ungraded groups?
How are students grouped within classes?
Homogeneously?
Heterogeneously?
Into reading groups?
Math groups?
Social studies groups?
Interest groups?

Curriculum

What is the curriculum organization?
Are there printed curriculum documents in use?
How carefully are the curriculum documents followed?
Do teachers make broad plans for a year's study?
How much deviation from formal curriculum is permitted?

Teaching Methods and Approaches

What instructional methods are favored by teachers?
Lectures?
Demonstrations?
Discussion?
Drill?
Field trips?
Games?
Role-playing?
Learning centers?
Individual projects?
What approaches are favored?
Expository?
Inquiry?

These broad questions are intended only as examples of the kinds of issues that must be considered in the development of any instructional plan. Unfortunately, it is impossible to provide a more specific, sequential, step-by-step listing of the instructional variables that must be considered in planning media skills instruction. Since teachers plan and execute instruction very differently, the integration of media skills instruction into classroom studies must conform to those individual teaching differences, and any description of that process must proceed by example.

In each of the examples that follow, all of which involve instruction in dictionary skills, a chronological narrative of the planning and teaching process is provided on the right side of the page and the pertinent instructional variable on the left.

Example One

Instructional Variable	Narrative
Community, Student Body	Ludwig van Beethoven School is an old, traditionally-designed building in a blue-collar neighborhood with decreasing property values and an increasing crime rate. Though there is some feeling of community in the neighborhood, that feeling has been on the wane. Nevertheless, the school has an active P.T.A., which has decided to stress, along with the school staff, a program designed to promote "working together and getting along with others." This program includes classroom emphasis on cooperation (e.g., increased use of group activities) and P.T.A.-sponsored activities (e.g., a weekend clean-up campaign involving groups of students and P.T.A. sponsors).
Facility (Media Center) Staff (Media Specialist) School Organization and Scheduling	Owing to a declining student enrollment, four years ago an empty classroom was remodelled to serve as a media center. A previously part-time media specialist was hired on a full-time basis. At first, classes were scheduled into the media center weekly for a "library" period, but as time went on the media specialist was able to convince the teaching staff to operate somewhat more flexibly (i.e., to bring classes to the media center for a particular purpose on a pre-planned basis), though teachers still maintain a fixed, weekly schedule.
Staff (Principal)	The principal, though traditional, supports a more flexible schedule for the media center and has indicated his support to teachers. Through extensive discussions with the media specialist, he now believes that an integrated program of media skills instruction would be of great benefit to students and has urged teachers to cooperate with the media specialist in this program.

Example One (cont'd)

Instructional Variable	Narrative
Staff (Teachers)	The teaching staff at Ludwig van Beethoven is traditional, and there is little attempt at team teaching. Pencil and paper exercises, lectures, demonstrations, and some discussions and group projects are the predominant teaching methods. Owing to the P.T.A.-staff program of encouraging "cooperation," more emphasis is now being placed on group activities. Teacher planning time is limited, and is restricted to before school, after school, and lunch time.
Staff (Third Grade Teacher) Teaching Methods and Approaches	One third-grade teacher at the school is typical of the teachers: she is a traditional teacher who favors expository teaching techniques, though she is cooperating with the P.T.A.-staff project and using more group activities than previously. She has recently read Glasser's *Schools without Failure* and is making some tentative attempts to use his reinforcement techniques.
Curriculum	One day, the media specialist and the teacher were having lunch together, one of the few times during the day available for planning. The teacher mentioned that her third grade class was going to be working on dictionary skills (part of the language arts and reading curriculum) and would like the media specialist to help.
Student Body (Achievement levels) Student Body (Abilities, interests)	The media specialist knew that the teacher's students had been exposed to the alphabetizing skills necessary for dictionary use, since she and the teacher had devised alphabetizing games which were used both in the classroom and in the media center. She knew that of the 28 children, two could alphabetize only to the first letter of a word (with difficulty), four could alphabetize to the second letter, seven could alphabetize to the third letter, and the rest could alphabetize to the end of the word. The media specialist also knew from previous experience with the teacher and her class that the teacher was effective and that most of the students were motivated and cooperative. There were only three exceptions—one student had a very short attention span and was hyperactive; two others were aggressive and frequently had to be separated from other students.

Example One (cont'd)

Instructional Variable	Narrative
	Both the media specialist and the teacher had kept records of student progress in alphabetizing and had noticed that success in alphabetizing correlated with student reading levels.
Curriculum (Media Skills) (Classroom) School Organization and Scheduling Curriculum (Media Skills and Classroom) Teaching Methods and Approaches	In thinking about how she might help in the dictionary unit, the media specialist considered a number of factors. First, the media specialist recognized that dictionary skills were a part of a sequence of instructional objectives for media skills that she had developed, and she was happy that those objectives might be integrated into a classroom language arts unit. She also realized that the need for dictionary skills was so ubiquitous that the objectives might also be related to another classroom unit—perhaps the science unit on astronomy currently under way. This was, moreover, another opportunity for the media specialist to move away from rigid "library" periods toward more flexible scheduling, and might, if learning activities were properly designed, also correspond with the P.T.A.-staff emphasis on group cooperation. The media specialist decided to suggest to the teacher that student groups prepare hand-bound astronomy dictionaries. Such a project would accomplish instructional objectives in media skills, language arts, and science and would encourage group cooperation.
Student Body (Grouping)	The media specialist and teacher discussed the project after school, and the teacher became enthusiastic after some initial hesitation. It was decided to place students in groups which would contain both children who were very good at alphabetizing and those who were less adept, thereby insuring the probable success of each group. As a result of a cooperative group effort, a tangible product would be created (bound dictionary).
Teaching Methods and Approaches	A collection of astronomy books and nonprint materials was sent from the media center to the third-grade classroom. Students were each asked to select five astronomical terms from the materials, write them on 3x5-inch slips of paper, and place each of them in one of 26 boxes (one for each letter of the alphabet) according to the first letter of the

Example One (cont'd)

Instructional Variable	Narrative

Student Body
(Grouping)

selected words. Student groups were assigned particular boxes and were asked, for each box, to look up the words in the dictionary (using dictionary skills learned in language arts), check spelling and syllabication, write definitions, write words in a sentence, and alphabetize the word groups. After the words were in order, the teacher and media specialist typed the words, leaving space for illustrations. Student groups were then asked to illustrate the words they had defined and alphabetized, each student in the group doing at least one illustration. The media specialist then took the resulting pages, and in a demonstration before the entire class, bound the book, which was subsequently added to the media center reference collection.

Student Body

Teaching Methods

School Organization and Scheduling

Teaching Methods and Approaches
(Activities)

All children participated in the activity and contributed initial terms, definitions, and illustrations. The teacher had introduced the activity, taught dictionary skills in the language arts period, and provided time during language arts and science periods for student groups to go to the media center to work on their dictionary projects. The media specialist gave supplementary lessons in dictionary skills, and assisted student groups in alphabetizing, locating definitions, and binding the finished book.

(Evaluation)

Evaluation of student progress was a simple matter of determining:
1) individual student contribution of initial words and later, illustrations
2) participation of each child in the group effort at alphabetizing, location of definitions, etc.
3) the quality of the finished product (i.e., in proper order, correct definition, appropriate illustrations, etc.).

Example Two

Instructional Variable	Narrative
Community	Bela Bartok School is a recently built school of modern design in a suburban community. Although
Facility	it has an enclosed media center, classrooms radiate out from the media center in three pods of four classrooms each (Pod I, K-2; Pod II, 3-4; Pod III, 5-6). Classrooms are semi-enclosed, with folding doors between rooms which may be opened for team teaching when required.
School Organization and Scheduling	Classes are graded, but there is considerable grouping and class changing within pods.

Pod II is composed of two third grades and two fourth grades. Teacher One has a third grade of 28 students; Teacher Two has a third grade of 27 students; Teacher Three has a fourth grade of 26 students; and Teacher Four has a fourth grade of 26 students. All classes change for math (by ability groups).

Teacher One and Teacher Two teach science and social studies to their own classes, closely following the curriculum. Teacher Three and Teacher Four team teach those subjects. All classes change for reading and are grouped by reading level as follows:

Teacher One
Group of reading level 3^2 students (20 students, subdivided)
Group of reading level 1^2 students (4 students)

Teacher Two
Group of reading level 2^1 students (9 students)
Group of reading level 3^1 students (18 students)

Teacher Three
Group of reading level 4 students (24 students, subdivided)

Teacher Four
Group of reading level 2^2 students (12 students)
Group of reading level 5 students (10 students)
Group of reading level 6 students (7 students)

Children on the primer or pre-primer level are kept by their home teacher for special help, and Teacher One, Teacher Two, and Teacher Three each have one child in this category.

Instructional Variable labels in left column (continued): Student Body (Achievement levels); Teaching Methods and Approaches; Student Body (Achievement levels); School Organization and Scheduling

Example Two (cont'd)

Instructional Variable	Narrative

Teaching Methods and Approaches

All teachers use the Ginn 360 series, although primer and pre-primer children are given special help with the Scott-Foresman reading series. Teacher One and Teacher Three use all of the SRA reading kits extensively.

Student Body
   (Achievement
   levels)

The students in Pod II had been introduced to dictionary skills by the teachers, but the media specialist had noticed that although students could talk about the dictionary, they had difficulty using it to locate specific words. When the media specialist attended the weekly after-school planning meeting of Pod II teachers, he mentioned his observation regarding dictionary skills, and the teachers agreed that although dictionary skills had been introduced, students probably needed more practice. The media specialist therefore devised a pre-test on the following dictionary skills:

a. finding definitions
b. use of guide words
c. syllabication
d. pronunciation
e. parts of speech
f. root words

The results of the pre-test indicated that student attainment of dictionary skills was closely related to their reading level: pre-primer-1^2 level students needed practice in all items; 2^1–3^2-level students needed practice in items b–f; 4-level students needed practice in items c–f; 5-level students needed practice in items d–f; and 6-level students needed practice only on items e–f. The

Teaching Methods and Approaches
   (Activities)

teachers and media specialist therefore decided to set up seven learning centers in the media center, one corresponding to each of the items on the pre-test, plus one additional center on picture dictionaries for children at the pre-primer and primer level. Students were sent to the media center by reading groups to work on the centers.

Students were accustomed to working with learning centers, since they had had prior experience of this kind both in their classrooms and in the media center. When they arrived by reading groups they were told individually which centers they needed to

Example Two (cont'd)

Instructional Variable	Narrative
	use based on their pre-test results. They worked on appropriate centers that day and on subsequent days, keeping a record of centers they had completed on a 3x5-inch card. Since all centers were self-contained (involving tape-recorded instructions and dittoed work sheets) students needed little assistance. However, the media specialist scheduled his time so that he would be available in the event that students needed his help.
(Evaluation)	During the course of four weeks, all Pod II students had completed those centers indicated by their pre-test. A post-test was administered by the teachers after that time.

Example Three

Instructional Variable	Narrative
Community Facility	John Lennon School is a new, open school in a suburban community. Class areas are divisible by moveable partitions, but are usually left open. A centrally located media center is separated from class areas only by shelving units.
Staff School Organization	Teachers are assigned a home room but do not necessarily teach on grade levels. Rather, they work as an upper team, middle team, and primary team. Within each team, teachers teach by subject (one handling reading and language arts, the others taking responsibility for math, science, and social studies, respectively). The media specialist works closely with each team.
Teaching Methods and Approaches	Though a wide range of teaching methods are employed, teachers especially favor programmed instruction and learning centers; contracting (i.e., forming "contracts" with students in which the students agree to undertake specific learning activities within specified time limits) is frequently used as an auxiliary technique.

Example Three (cont'd)

Instructional Variables	Narrative

Student Body
(Ability level)

The reading/language arts teacher of the middle cluster was preparing to undertake a unit on dictionary skills with her 20 students (one class), all of whom were at reading level 3^1 to 3^2, though their nominal grade levels varied from two to four. Before beginning the unit, the teacher met with the media specialist and the two developed eight instructional objectives for the unit. The students would be required to:

Teaching Methods and
Approaches
(Objectives)

1. Identify and locate dictionaries.
2. Select dictionaries to find the meaning of a word.
3. Select dictionaries for the purpose of finding the correct pronunciation of words, word derivations, parts of speech, multiple word meanings, and syllabication.
4. Alphabetize to the end of words.
5. Identify and locate guide words.
6. Locate specific words in a dictionary.
7. Find specific information in materials using guide words.
8. Use a dictionary to find the meaning, part of speech, derivation, syllabication, and pronunciation of a word.

(Activities)

The teacher and media specialist developed a series of activity cards for each objective. Each card was related to the dictionary skill objectives but also to other units that the students were studying at the same time (e.g., transportation, plants). For example, one activity card for objective 5 was accompanied by ten plastic models of various transportation devices (car, plane, rocket, truck, motorcycle, train, bus, horse, wagon, chariot). The card instructed students to identify the transportation device represented by the model, find the name of the device in the dictionary, and list the guide words on the page on which the name of the device was found.

(Pre-testing)

Since the teacher and media specialist had recently taught lessons on alphabetizing to the students, they did not feel that a pre-test on alphabetizing was necessary. The teacher taught an initial lesson on the dictionary and students were then asked to

Example Three (cont'd)

Instructional Variables	Narrative
(Contracting)	accept contracts for activity cards of their choice related to each of the eight objectives. Some activity cards required media center activities supervised by the media specialist and others required classroom activities supervised by the teacher. Students had a choice of at least three activity cards for each objective.
(Lecture/ discussion)	The teacher's initial lesson was a lecture/discussion in which she brought in a large, covered basket with a dictionary inside. She told the students that she had put 30,000 words into the basket, and the class discussed whether such a thing was possible and how it might be done. They discussed the problems that might arise in locating one particular word if each word were written on a little card. Generally dictionaries were discussed—their purpose, arrangement, and use. The teacher then introduced the activity cards, and students were asked to contract for those activities in each group which they wanted to perform. Each child had a checklist of activities and as each was completed correctly, it was initialed by the teacher or media specialist. A certain time period each day was set aside for work on the activity cards, and the media specialist therefore planned to be available in the media center at that time to assist children working on activity cards requiring use of the media center.
(Evaluation)	Evaluation of student performance was made by examining the checklists to see if students had successfully completed all contracted activities, and by the administration of a short, written test by the teacher.

PLANNING UNITS OF MEDIA SKILLS INSTRUCTION

The foregoing listing of instructional methods and variables, together with the examples of teaching media skills in three divergent situations, suggests an elaboration of the simple model of media skills instruction presented in Chapter 1 (Figure 8, page 22). The simple model was comprised of five basic steps:

1. the formulation of a sequence of classroom instructional objectives by the teacher and a sequence of media skills objectives by the media specialist;

2.   the merging of classroom instructional objectives and media skills objectives into a single set of unit objectives;
3.   the planning and implementation of teaching activities;
4.   assessment of student performance;
5.   revision of unit for future use.

A more complex but realistic model might consist of 13 steps:

Step One: Identification of Content

Teachers identify the subject content for a year's classroom instruction, though that content may be specified in written curriculum documents. Media specialists identify media skills content for each year of instruction. For any given unit of instruction, specific subject content and media skills content is jointly determined by teachers and media specialists, though the teacher may take primary responsibility for subject content and the media specialist for media skills content.

Joint planning of unit content is essential in order to insure the operational interdependence of subject matter and media skills. For instance, in example one above, it is difficult to imagine how subjects as ostensibly different as astronomy and dictionary skills might have been operationally combined without joint planning of unit content.

Step Two: Specification of Unit Objectives

As in the case of identifying content, teachers develop classroom instructional objectives and media specialists develop a sequence of media skills objectives. However, in specifying instructional objectives for a particular unit, the two must be merged, again for the purpose of insuring the operational interdependence of subject matter and media skills.

Step Three: Examination of Available Resources

Once content and objectives for a unit have been specified, available instructional materials related to the content must be examined. The availability or lack of such resources may influence the choice of instructional methods or may indicate a need to develop original teaching materials.

Step Four: Pre-testing

Prior to undertaking a unit, it is essential to find out:

1.   If the students have previously learned skills necessary to the mastery of the new content ("entry behavior").
2.   How much of the new content students already know ("terminal behavior").

Pre-testing need not be formal. It may take the form of games, puzzles, contests, or simple oral questions, or it may be omitted altogether if entry and terminal behaviors are already clearly known by the teacher or media specialist. For example, if alphabetizing skills (an entry behavior necessary for learning dictionary skills) have just been taught and assessed prior to undertaking a unit on dictionary skills, it may not be necessary to pre-test again for alphabetizing skills.

It is desirable when pre-testing terminal behaviors to assess as many discrete components of the new content or skill as possible, since students may already know some components and not others. For instance, in example two above, six components of terminal behavior in dictionary skills were pre-tested (definitions, guide words, syllabication, pronunciation, parts of speech, root words), and it was discovered that nearly all students already knew some components and not others. It was therefore possible to tailor learning activities to specific individual needs.

Step Five: Development of Unit Strategy

It is in the development of a unit strategy—that is, the selection of teaching method or methods—that instructional methods appropriate to teaching specific content are examined in relation to the entire range of variables in the school environment. As indicated in the three examples above, the process of selecting methods is not amenable to step-by-step analysis since it is influenced by many fortuitous factors (e.g., the preferences of teachers, physical facilities, student attitudes, etc.). One method of teaching dictionary skills may be entirely appropriate to one school environment and entirely inappropriate to another. Bela Bartok School's learning centers were very effective in a school environment in which learning centers were encouraged and students had had wide experience with them, but they might well have failed at Ludwig van Beethoven School. Selection of methods and strategies for media skills instruction therefore depends upon:

1. a thorough knowledge of the instructional and environmental variables of the school;
2. joint planning of unit strategies by teachers and media specialists so that the methods chosen are both mutually acceptable and consistent with instructional variables.

Step Six: Determination of Instructional Responsibilities

Since media skills instruction is a mutual undertaking of teachers and media specialists, it is important to determine for any unit the instructional role of each staff member. Will initial instruction be done in the classroom by the teacher with follow-up activities in the media center, or vice versa? Will the entire unit be team-taught, partly team-taught, or will the media specialist teach some activities while the teacher teaches others?

Step Seven: Determination of Student Groupings

Will instruction be given to the entire class at once or will students be asked to do individual or group work? If students are to be grouped for instruction, how will the grouping be done? Homogeneously? Heterogeneously? By reading groups?

Step Eight: Selection of Resources

Though resources should have been examined prior to determining strategies and methods, appropriate resources and materials must now be selected for actual use. If a learning center approach to teaching dictionary skills has been selected, for example, a set of expository-type transparencies on dictionary skills may not be useful. Instead, original learning centers may have to be designed and constructed before the unit can be implemented.

Step Nine: Allocation of Time

Some flexibility in the allocation of time limits to each section of the unit is desirable, since it is often difficult to predetermine how long it will take students to accomplish planned activities unless the unit has been previously taught. Nevertheless, time limits must be determined as carefully as possible in order for teachers and media specialists to schedule their own participation in instructional activities, and to insure the completion of the unit in a reasonable, often fixed, time period (e.g., one grading period).

Step Ten: Allocation of Space

Will instruction take place in the classroom? In the media center? Do the methods chosen require that instructional materials or learning centers be permanently set up in some fixed location? Will these materials or centers interfere with other activities in those locations?

Step Eleven: Implementation of Unit

After planning it, do it.

Step Twelve: Evaluation of Exit Behaviors
(Post-testing)

After all activities have been completed, student performance must be assessed. This process will be examined in detail in Chapter 4.

Step Thirteen: Revision of Unit

As a final step, the unit must be revised for future use on the basis of:

1. How successfully chosen methods produced desired student outcomes.
2. How easily and smoothly each step in the instructional process was completed (pre-testing, methods used, student groupings, division

of instructional responsibility, time limits, space allocations, resources used, assessment measures used).

Not all of the 13 steps in the planning and execution of media skills units are uniformly applicable in every school environment, and the chronological order of the steps may vary with each unique situation. But all steps play an important part in developing units of instruction and must be considered at some point in the planning process.

PLANNING MEDIA SKILLS LESSONS

Planning individual media skills lessons within a unit is very similar to planning units. It includes:

1. Development of precise **performance objectives** which directly relate appropriate media skills to the subject matter of the classroom instructional unit and which specify observable student behaviors, conditions of performance, and performance criteria (see Chapter 2).
2. Development of a **lesson strategy**, which includes an initiating activity (an opening activity designed to spark immediate interest in the lesson), developmental activities (activities designed to outline the major components of the primary learning experience), and the primary method or activity;
3. Selection of appropriate **instructional materials** and resources;
4. **Scheduling** of classes or groups of students;
5. Establishment of **time limits** for the completion of the lesson;
6. Allocation of the **space** in which the lesson will be taught;
7. **Evaluation** of student performance;
8. **Revision** of the lesson for future use.

One sample lesson plan which integrates teaching the use of the card catalog into a fourth-grade social studies unit on the Civil War may illustrate these eight components of lesson plan design.

Performance Objectives:
1. Students will identify the card catalog and give a brief oral description of its purpose and arrangement.
2. Given a written list of subjects, authors, and titles related to the Civil War, students will identify the card catalog drawer number in which the appropriate subject, author, or title may be found with 75 percent accuracy.

Initiating Activity:
Question: Who knows what this is? (Hold up a door key.)
Response: Key
Question: What kinds of things have keys?
Responses: Cars, doors, pianos, music, maps, etc.
Question: What do keys do?
Responses: Open or close, lock or unlock, provide access, something that explains or solves something else (as in the "key" to a mystery), etc.

Question: Can you think of a special key that we have in the media center?
Response: card catalog.

Development Activities (lecture—discussion):

Today we are going to look at this special key (indicate card catalog). Why do you suppose we call it the key to the materials in the media center?
Response: (Variable).

If you were hungry and the door to the refrigerator was locked, it wouldn't do you much good, would it?
Response: (Variable).

So, we need a way to use all the materials in the media center—to eat up all the words with our eyes and the sounds with our ears. The card catalog opens up the materials to use. It:

helps us find materials
provides access to materials
holds all the materials together so that we have only one place
  that we have to look for them
helps us solve problems by locating materials for us

Now, how do you suppose we use this special tool?
1. It is in alphabetical order.
2. It contains drawers which start at the top and work down, and then go from left to right (demonstrate).
3. It contains a card for every resource in the media center by
    a. author
    b. title
    c. subject

Since it is in alphabetical order, what do you suppose I would do to find a book about clothing worn during the Civil War?, etc.

Activity:

Given a list of twenty subjects, authors, and titles related to the Civil War, students will identify specific drawers in the card catalog where material may be found.

Materials:

Students must sit near the card catalog, but the only material required is the activity list of subjects, authors, and titles.

Scheduling:

Lesson takes place with half a class at once (15 students) in the media center during two 40-minute time periods as scheduled with the teacher.

Evaluation:

Students will complete the activity with no more than five mistakes in the twenty items, with no fewer than 26 of the 30 students attaining this level of performance.

Lesson Revision:
>No revision appeared necessary, since all students attained the specified performance and no difficulties in scheduling or execution of the lesson were encountered.

SUMMARY

All of the techniques and methods of modern instruction—lecture, discussion, demonstration, drill, field trips, role-playing, games, audiovisual instruction, reading, individual or group study, programmed instruction, and learning centers—may be useful in teaching media skills. However, owing to the necessity for integrating media skills teaching into everyday classroom teaching, the many variables in any instructional environment must play an important part in the selection of an instructional method.

Choice of teaching methods is only one of many steps in the process of planning units that incorporate media skills instruction, a process which also includes: planning unit content; specifying objectives; examining available resources; pre-testing; developing unit strategy; determining instructional responsibilities; determining student groupings; selecting of resources; allocating time and space; implementing the unit; evaluating exit behavior; and, revising the unit. Lesson planning is a similar process; it includes specifying performance objectives, developing lesson strategy, selecting instructional resources, scheduling students, allocating time and space, evaluating student performance, and revising the unit for future use.

NOTES

[1] See, for example, V. S. Gerlach and D. P. Ely, *Teaching and Media: A Systematic Approach* (Englewood Cliffs, N.J., Prentice-Hall, Inc., 1971).

BIBLIOGRAPHY

Blanc, S. S. "Planning a Teaching Unit for the Primary Grades." *Science and Children* 9:7 (April 1972), pp. 21-24.

Brown, James W.; Lewis, Richard B.; and Harcleroad, Fred F. *AV Instruction: Media and Methods.* New York, McGraw-Hill, 1969.

Franklin, M. P., ed. *School Organization: Theory and Practice.* Chicago, Rand McNally, 1967.

Gagné, R. M. *The Conditions of Learning.* 2nd ed. New York, Holt, Rinehart, and Winston, 1970.

Gerlach, Vernon S., and Ely, Donald P. *Teaching and Media: A Systematic Approach.* Englewood Cliffs, N.J., Prentice-Hall, 1971.

Harrell, Roger L. "G-C-O-LP-G: An Instructional Development Plan." *Education* 93:1 (September-October, 1972), pp. 94-100.

Howes, Virgil M. *Individualization of Instruction.* New York, Macmillan, 1970.

Hyman, Ronald T. *Ways of Teaching.* New York, Lippincott, 1970.

Joyce, Bruce R., and Harootunian, Berj. *The Structure of Teaching.* Chicago, Science Research Associates, 1967.

Kibler, Robert J.; Cegala, Donald J.; Barker, Larry L.; and Miles, David T. *Objectives for Instruction and Evaluation.* Boston, Allyn and Bacon, 1974.

Margrabe, Mary. *The "Now" Library.* Washington, D.C., Acropolis Books, 1973.

National Council for the Social Studies. *How to Teach Library Research Skills in Secondary School Social Studies.* Arlington, Va., National Council for the Social Studies, National Education Association, 1968.

Owens, R. G. *Organizational Behavior in Schools.* Englewood Cliffs, N.J., Prentice-Hall, 1970.

Voight, Ralph C. *Invitation to Learning: The Learning Center Handbook.* Washington, D.C., Acropolis Books, 1971.

CHAPTER 4

EVALUATION OF STUDENT PERFORMANCE
IN MEDIA SKILLS

PRINCIPLES OF ASSESSMENT

Evaluation of student performance in media skills is much like evaluation of student performance in any other subject of study. Several general principles apply:

1. It is essential that students know from the onset that they *will* be evaluated, how they will be evaluated, and how the evaluation will affect the reporting of their performance.
2. Tests or other assessment measures must be precisely matched to instructional objectives and learning activities. It is unreasonable to test what has not been taught.
3. Different kinds of instructional objectives and activities require different evaluation techniques. Pencil-and-paper tests may be fine for assessing verbal learning, for example, but learning of manipulative skills may require assessment through direct observation or some other means.
4. Assessment instruments need not be designed to torture the student. Games and puzzles are just as effective for evaluative purposes as formal written tests.

Evaluation and Media Skills

Though evaluation of student performance in media skills must conform to these general principles of assessment, it is not quite as straightforward as classroom evaluation. In the classroom instructional model, instructional objectives are formulated, teaching methods chosen, learning activities undertaken, student performance assessed, and the results of assessment reported. In the integrated model of media skills instruction (see Chapter 1), media skills objectives are integrated into classroom units and instructional activities are keyed directly to classroom activities. Similarly, evaluation of student performance in media skills must be integrated into the evaluation of student performance in classroom lessons and units, and must become a part of any reporting of student progress. If a student receives an "A" on a particular social studies unit, it must be not only because he mastered the unit objectives related to content, but also because he mastered those media skills objectives integrated into the social studies unit. Students must be made aware of the fact that their performance in media skills activities is an essential part of their classroom performance and will be included in any reporting of classroom progress.

Clearly, all the variables in the school environment cited in Chapter 3 apply to evaluation just as they do to instruction. In particular, teacher preferences in techniques of evaluation, grading, and reporting become exceedingly important, since evaluation of student progress in media skills must be integrated into the classroom evaluative framework.

Two Kinds of Evaluation

There has been considerable recent discussion among educators regarding the relative merits of two systems of evaluating student performance: **norm-referenced evaluation** and **criterion-referenced evaluation.**

Norm-referenced evaluation systems compare one student's performance on tests or other assessment measures to the performance of all other students in the class—the familiar "grading-on-a-curve." Though students often favor this system, owing to the fact that it depends upon group competition rather than complete subject mastery, its weakness is the very fact that it does *not* require subject mastery. It is quite possible, for example, that a student might receive an "A" on a test which indicates that he has mastered only 20 percent of the subject content, provided that the majority of his peers mastered *less* than 20 percent of the content. Norm-referenced evaluation does not require any fixed level of performance, but rather judges each student's performance in relation to the average performance of the group or class.

Criterion-referenced evaluation is quite a different matter. The instructor begins with the formulation of a precise set of instructional objectives, which include criteria of acceptable performance, in accordance with Robert Mager's specifications for the design of instructional objectives (see Chapter 2). Learning activities are keyed directly to objectives, and evaluation is a simple matter of determining whether or not the student has attained specified criteria of mastery. There is no invidious comparison of students. Each student either attains the mastery criteria, or he does not. If he does not, then additional learning activities must be provided until he *does* attain the criteria.

Since criterion-referenced evaluation requires a minimum standard of student performance, it is especially useful for educators and educational systems willing to be held accountable for a specified level of student learning. Such educators or educational systems may clearly specify to the parents and community the instructional objectives that students will be asked to master and, through criterion-referenced testing, may demonstrate student attainment of those objectives. Owing to such obvious advantages, "mastery learning" and criterion-referenced evaluation are rapidly gaining wide acceptance in the educational community.

Criterion-Referenced Evaluation and Media Skills

Criterion-referenced evaluation is especially suitable for use in a system of media skills instruction which follows the integrated model recommended in this book. The following are among the advantages of a criterion-referenced system:

1. The integrated model of media skills instruction is predicated on a sequence of precise instructional objectives, and on performance objectives incorporating specific criteria of mastery for units and lessons (see Chapter 2). It is therefore a relatively simple matter for teachers and media specialists to devise assessment measures that test student attainment of the objectives at the specified level of mastery.

2. Criterion-referenced evaluation of student performance in media skills is easy to integrate into *any* system of classroom evaluation. Either the student attains media skills objectives or he does not. If he does not, additional learning activities may be prepared for him until he *does*. He simply has not completed his classroom instructional unit until he has mastered the media skills objectives at the specified level.
3. Criterion-referenced evaluation instruments may serve a variety of useful purposes. Since they are precisely keyed to objectives, they may be used just as easily for pre-testing as for post-testing. Moreover, since student attainment of each objective in the sequence of media skills objectives will be tested, the totality of test results will provide a clear indication of the effectiveness of the media skills program as a whole.

The key to success in the use of criterion-referenced evaluation is obviously the careful design of instructional objectives and the precise matching of assessment measures or tests to objectives. Consider the following example:

Objective: The student will operate a reel-to-reel tape recorder to play a pre-recorded audio tape, with no operational errors.

Test Item: On the diagram of a tape recorder below, label the parts of the recorder, including the volume control and the function lever.

Clearly, the objective and the test item do *not* match, since the objective only requires operational mastery of the playing function of a tape recorder, whereas the test item requires an entirely different skill (i.e., recall of terminology). It is difficult, in fact, to imagine a written test item that would adequately assess the stated objective. Direct teacher observation of student performance is required.

The foregoing example illustrates an egregious matching error, whereas such errors are usually more subtle. For example:

Objective: The student will identify all main headings and sub-headings in an encyclopedia article.

Test Item: Examine the following copy of an article from the *World Book Encyclopedia.* Underline each main heading with a single line and each sub-heading with a double line. Explain in a few sentences the difference between main headings and sub-headings.

The test item is fine, until it asks for an explanation. The objective requires only identification, not explanation. If an explanation is to be required, the objective must be modified accordingly.

Objective: The student will identify all main headings and sub-headings in an encyclopedia article and in a few short sentences, explain the difference between the two.

Constructing Written Test Items

Matching test items to objectives is largely a matter of *what* to ask—that is, the content of the questions. As the foregoing examples illustrate, test items should ask neither more nor less than the objective specifies. Once the content of questions has been determined, however, they must be cast into some particular form: essay, matching, multiple-choice, true-false, completion, short answer, etc.

Essay test items are ostensibly the easiest for the instructor to devise, but they are certainly the most difficult for the student to answer, particularly at the elementary level, because they require a high level of both reading comprehension and organized writing. It is certainly preferable, especially for primary grade students, to couch essay questions in terms that require the least interpretive ability in reading and writing ("name, state, outline, summarize, put in your own words" as opposed to "interpret, discuss, compare, contrast, criticize"). Thus, for the objective "students will explain the difference between main headings and sub-headings in an encyclopedia article," the essay test item "in your own words, tell the difference between a main heading and a sub-heading in an encyclopedia" is preferable to "compare and contrast main headings and sub-headings in an encyclopedia." But even when the simpler forms of essay questions are chosen, they are only marginally appropriate for many if not most kinds of subject matter in the elementary school, and they should be used judiciously.

Perhaps a better way to assess knowledge of the same kinds of information is the short-answer or completion item, which provides a definition or description and requires the student to write the defined or described terms.

Example: The title page of the book usually includes a _____,
_____ , _____ , and
_____ .

The title page of a book contains four kinds of information. What are these four kinds?

1. _____
2. _____
3. _____
4. _____

Though such items do not test "critical thinking"—a quality often imputed to essay tests—they do, when carefully designed, provide an excellent assessment of objective knowledge.

Test items involving the matching of terms go a step further than completion items, for they require that students draw logical connections between terms rather than simply recall unrelated bits of information. Yet, such items do not require the complex ability to construct and order sentences, as do essay questions, so they are more appropriate for use in primary grades.

Example: Match the following words and draw lines between the words that match:

fiction   alphabetical order
non-fiction   vertical file
index   factual
pamphlet   imaginary

Multiple-choice and true-false test items often seem the simplest form of assessment, but in fact they are more difficult than short answer/completion items since they require the logical and systematic elimination (or identification) of incorrect answers. In addition, the instructor is *trying* to be "tricky" in order to tempt students with answers that are close to the truth, but not true, thereby forcing careful thought. It is not advisable, however, to be *too* tricky. For example, it is unfair to pose a true-false question such as "Encyclopedias are always arranged alphabetically" unless information regarding encyclopedias with non-alphabetical arrangement has been carefully taught (*not* casually mentioned).

In choosing various items for a written test, it is advisable to follow this procedure:

1. Keep a daily inventory of possible test items as each lesson is presented, including a variety of item types (multiple choice, matching, true-false, etc.).
2. Select the best of the items in the inventory and prepare a rough draft of the test.
3. Prepare a final draft of the test, arranging similar item types together, placing items and types in ascending order of difficulty, and varying the pattern or sequence of correct responses.

Observation as an Evaluation Technique

As indicated earlier in this chapter, many kinds of learning are not amenable to written testing of any kind. Included in this category are many media skills, particularly those related to location, operation, and manipulation, which must be assessed by direct observation of student performance rather than by written test items.

In observing student performance, several considerations are of importance:

1. Just as in written test items, observation of student performance must be *directly* related to stated objectives. If the stated objective is "the student will operate a reel-to-reel tape recorder to play a pre-recorded audio tape, with no operational errors," then any tape recorder operations unrelated to playing pre-recorded tapes (i.e., microphone operation, record-mode operation, etc.) should be disregarded. Only those observed aspects of student performance directly related to the objective are of importance to the evaluation.
2. Though observed aspects of student performance unrelated to the stated objective should be disregarded, *every* aspect of student performance related to the objective should be carefully observed and evaluated. Thus, for the objective above, *all* aspects of the playing operation of tape recorders are implicit in the objective and should be part of the observational assessment (i.e., turning on power, threading tape, activating play mode, adjusting volume, etc.).
3. In addition to the major behavioral aspects of student performance, subtleties such as hesitations, false starts, and so forth should be carefully noted. A student may "pass" despite hesitations and false

starts, but such behavior indicates a need for additional learning activities, practice, and reinforcement.

A Note on Commercial Tests of Media Skills

In an objective-based system of instruction, it is *always* preferable to design original tests that exactly assess stated objectives. However, it may be informative for the media specialist to examine several commercial tests for comparative purposes. A brief bibliography of commercial library and media skills tests is therefore appended to this chapter.

SUMMARY

Evaluation of student performance in media skills is much like evaluation of student performance in any other subject of study. Proper evaluative practice therefore involves:

1. informing students in advance of the evaluation technique to be used, and of the way in which the results of evaluation will affect the reporting of their performance;
2. precise matching of assessment measures to instructional objectives;
3. choice of appropriate evaluation techniques;
4. choice, if possible, of an evaluation technique that is not torturous for the student.

Criterion-referenced evaluation techniques are particularly useful in the integrated model of media skills instruction, since that model is predicated on a sequence of precise instructional objectives. In addition, the results of criterion-referenced evaluation of media skills performance may easily be integrated into *any* classroom system of evaluation and reporting.

Careful formulation of written test items and observational techniques is essential in order to insure precise matching of objectives and assessments.

BIBLIOGRAPHY

Ahmann, J. Stanley, and Glock, Marvin D. *Evaluating Pupil Growth.* 5th ed. Boston, Allyn and Bacon, 1975.

Ahmann, J. Stanley, and Glock, Marvin D. *Measuring and Evaluating Educational Achievement.* Boston, Allyn and Bacon, 1971.

Block, J., ed. *Mastery Learning: Theory and Practice.* New York, Holt, Rinehart, and Winston, 1971.

Ebel, Robert L. *Measuring Educational Achievement.* Englewood Cliffs, N.J., Prentice-Hall, 1965.

Jackson, R. "Developing Criterion-Referenced Tests." *T.M. Reports*, No. 15. Princeton, N.J., Educational Testing Service, 1970.

Kibler, Robert J.; Cegala, Donald J.; Barker, Larry L.; and Miles, David T. *Objectives for Instruction and Evaluation.* Boston, Allyn and Bacon, 1974.

Livingston, S. A. *The Reliability of Criterion-Referenced Measures.* Baltimore, Md., Center for the Study of Social Organization of the Schools, Johns Hopkins University, 1970.

Popham, W. J., and Husek, T. R. "Implication of Criterion-Referenced Measurement." *Journal of Educational Measurements* 6:1 (Spring 1969), pp. 1-9.

Smythe, M. J.; Kibler, R. J.; and Hutchings, P. W. "A Comparison of Norm-Referenced and Criterion-Referenced Measurement with Implication for Communication Instruction." *The Speech Teacher* 22:1 (January 1973), pp. 1-17.

Thorndike, R. L., ed. *Educational Measurement.* Washington, D.C., American Council on Education, 1971.

Tests

The Iowa Tests of Basic Skills. Boston, Houghton Mifflin Company, 1971.

Library Tests 1-3. Logan, Iowa, Perfection Form Company, 1973.

National Test of Library Skills. Fort Lauderdale, Fla., American Testing Company, 1971.

Wisconsin Tests of Reading Skills Development: Study Skills. Minneapolis, Minn., NCS Interpretive Scoring Systems, 1973.

CHAPTER 5

IMPLEMENTING A MEDIA SKILLS PROGRAM

An instructional model, no matter how precise, can only approximate local school conditions. Implementation plans based on a particular model will therefore differ considerably from school to school and system to system.

System variables affecting the implementation of a media skills program are numerous and may be grouped into several broad categories.

SYSTEM VARIABLES

Staff Variables

The effectiveness of a media skills program and the speed with which it may be implemented is heavily dependent on both system-level and school-level staff. Is there a full-time media specialist assigned to each school? Does that media specialist have clerical or paraprofessional assistance, so that the pressure of clerical tasks does not impede the implementation of the new program? Does a system-level media or library supervisory staff exist to shoulder some of the burden of program development and the communication of program to subject supervisors, line administrative staff, and teachers?

Though it is not impossible for a part-time media specialist who has no clerical assistance and who works in a system with no media or library supervisor to develop and implement a media skills program, the program must perforce be less comprehensive and must be implemented over a longer period of time than in a system incorporating full-time media specialists, media clerks or paraprofessionals, and a media supervisory staff.

Organizational and Procedural Variables

Variables of organization and procedure in any school system profoundly affect the implementation of *any* new program. Must new school programs be subjected to a formal approval or adoption procedure? Once formally adopted, how are programs implemented? Is in-service training relating to the new program available for school staff, supervisory staff, and administrative staff? How much and what kind of supervisory support is available to insure comprehensive implementation? Do media supervisors meet regularly with subject supervisors and administrative staff to discuss new programs, thereby eliciting the support of subject supervisors and administrators in communicating the media skills program to teachers? Are teachers bound by written curriculum documents and, if so, can media skills objectives be incorporated into those documents? Is time available for the media supervisor to meet with individual media specialists or a committee of media specialists to discuss implementation plans?

As in the case of media center staffing, these and other related questions will in large measure determine the speed with which a media skills program can be implemented, as well as the ultimate scope and comprehensiveness of that program.

Media Services Variables

A media skills program is only one of the many services of the school media center. The evaluation and acquisition of instructional materials, assistance to students and staff in the use of those materials, media production services, reference services, bibliographic services, circulation control, and the myriad of other important media center services, are all closely related to a systematic program of media skills instruction and often may be integrated into such a program. Well-established, on-going services must be maintained, and maintaining these services may restrict the amount of time available for developing and implementing a media skills program. Nevertheless, with careful planning at both the system and school level, a media skills program may be instituted without seriously disturbing the on-going services of the school media center.

SYSTEM-LEVEL PLANNING

If a system-level supervisor or supervisory staff exists for media centers or school libraries, that staff must clearly play a vital role in the development and implementation of a media skills program. Supervisory efforts may proceed in seven stages:

Step One: Discussion Stage

The media or library supervisor must generate initial discussion of the prospective program with the media specialists, subject supervisors, and line administrators. Most school media specialists will quickly recognize and accept the broad goals and purposes of the program, since most will have been involved in some sort of media skills or library skills instruction. The program may therefore be presented by the supervisor as an effort to:

- systematize instructional objectives and techniques;
- integrate media skills objectives into classroom instructional units;
- elicit the support of subject supervisors, administrators, and teachers
- facilitate inter-school exchange of successful teaching materials, ideas, and approaches;
- provide in-service training in various aspects of the prospective program, and
- insure on-going supervisory support in the implementation process.

Discussions with subject supervisors and administrators should, where possible, link the prospective media skills program to other priority programs within the system: e.g., efforts to systematize and objectivize instruction in all subjects, efforts to improve student performance in basic skills (reading and mathematics), and so forth. Discussions should stress the support such a program might provide to classroom teaching, the cooperation between teacher and media specialist that is necessary for the success of the program, and the importance of media skills objectives for student performance in *all* subjects.

Step Two: Committee Formation

Following discussions with media specialists, subject supervisors, and administrators, the media supervisor should form and chair a committee of media specialists, with the representation of teachers, subject supervisors, and administrators, to develop a sequence of media skills objectives (perhaps using the objective suggested in Chapter 2 as a guide), sample instructional activities (see Part II of this book), a description of recommended teaching strategies (see Chapter 3), criterion-referenced assessment measures (see Chapter 4), and suggested in-service training activities.

Step Three: Adoption of Program

Once the program committee has finalized a set of objectives, prepared sample activities, and developed implementation strategies, the media supervisor should present the program for formal adoption by the school system. The process of adopting new instructional programs differs widely from school system to school system; it may involve anything from a simple endorsement by the school superintendent to a complex system of staff discussion, discussion and ratification by an instructional council (or executive staff), and endorsement by the school superintendent and board of education. Regardless of the nature of the adoption procedure, the media supervisor must not neglect this step, for it may weigh heavily in subsequent discussions with subject supervisors and school administrators during the implementation process.

Step Four: Integration of Objectives into Existing Curriculum

Because media skills objectives are not designed to be taught in isolation, the media supervisor should seek the incorporation of media skills objectives and recommended activities into the curriculum documents of *all* subject areas as those documents are revised or adopted.

Step Five: In-Service Activities

Once a sequence of objectives has been developed and formalized, in-service programs for media specialists—and, if practical, for teachers and administrators—may be planned to introduce the objectives and to suggest methods of implementation. Any in-service program should include sessions on all the major components of a media skills program: i.e., objectives, instructional methods, evaluation, and program implementation. Though a single sequence of objectives should be presented to media specialists to insure system-wide consistency, broad latitude in instructional methodology and implementation tactics must be encouraged owing to local school differences.

Step Six: On-going Supervisory Support

An on-going program of supervisory support should be provided to media specialists as they begin to implement a media skills program. Such support may be particularly effective if directed toward principals, since the support and encouragement of the principal may insure the full cooperation of the teaching staff—an essential ingredient in all successful programs of media skills instruction.

Step Seven: Revision of Program

As the media skills program is implemented, the media supervisor must continue to meet with the media skills committee and to visit individual media specialists in their schools in an on-going effort to revise, expand, and improve the media skills program.

SCHOOL-LEVEL PLANNING

The first step in implementing a media skills program at the school level is the formation of a sequence of instructional objectives. If a sequence of objectives has been developed at the system level, it may be modified to suit local school conditions. If no system-level sequence of objectives exists, such a sequence may be developed by the school media specialist, using the objectives suggested in Chapter 2 as a guide, and incorporating specific peculiarities of local school curriculum and instructional methodology.

Once a sequence of instructional objectives for media skills has been formulated or modified, it may be used by the media specialist in communicating to administrators and teachers the exact nature and content of the proposed media skills program. Subsequently, the objectives may be used by the media specialist and teachers as a planning guide for integrating media skills into classroom instructional units.

Before formally introducing a media skills program to the school principal and teaching staff, the media specialist must develop a profile of the school; this profile will include information related to each of the variables in the school environment outlined in Chapter 3. Such information will prove invaluable in developing with the faculty a rational approach to media skills instruction and will later be helpful in planning specific teaching units. A sample checklist that may be useful in preparing a school profile is presented in Figure 13, page 74.

Figure 13

School Profile Checklist

This checklist was designed for use in gathering information about your school, the surrounding community, the staff, and the student body. Most of this information is a necessary prerequisite to planning a media skills program with the principal and teaching staff.

A. Community
   1. Examine a map of the community which your school serves, noting:
       a. distances between houses
       b. types of dwellings, roads and traffic patterns, business areas, recreation areas, and distances students walk or travel by bus.
   2. Examine a local directory, noting:
       a. types of businesses in the community
       b. civic, social, and religious organizations.
   3. Examine past reports of the P.T.A. or other parent groups, noting:
       a. purposes and goals
       b. budget priorities
       c. P.T.A. committees
       d. active members.
   4. Examine records of past activity within the school by community volunteer groups.
   5. Read the local paper or newsletter for community events and information, noting:
       a. cultural opportunities
       b. recreational opportunities
       c. adult education opportunities
       d. community goals and priorities.
   6. Read the school annual reports for pertinent information about the community, noting, if available:
       a. family occupations
       b. educational backgrounds
       c. parent objectives
   7. Examine results of any past community survey.
   8. Talk with community members.

B. Student Body
   1. Read school annual reports for statistical information on the student body, noting:
       a. enrollment figures at various age levels
       b. multi-ethnic populations
       c. bi-lingual students
       d. special student populations (such as the handicapped, special education students, etc.)
       e. statistical summaries of test scores from national achievement tests
   2. Read student cumulative records.
       a. Identify scholarship records.
       b. Identify school progress.
       c. Note reading levels.
       d. Identify achievement, diagnostic, or intelligence test information.
       e. Note attendance record.
       f. Identify interests based on interest inventories.
       g. Read anecdotal records.
       h. Examine health records.
       i. Examine any student sample work, reading records, or autobiographical material.

Figure 13 (cont'd)

B.   Student Body (cont'd)
    3.   Talk with individual students.
    4.   Listen to teacher observations of student abilities.

C.   School Facility
    1.   Examine a blueprint or map of school; or
    2.   Walk around the building.
       a. Identify specific rooms.
       b. Note rooms which may be used for a variety of purposes.
       c. Note electrical outlets and lighting.
       d. Note space possibilities.
       e. Examine furniture and other available equipment.
       f. Note the traffic patterns and hallways.
       g. Note the position of the media center in relation to the class-rooms and other school areas.
       h. Note the position of telephones and television antenna outlets (if they exist).

D.   Instructional Staff
    1.   Examine the school annual report, noting:
       a. staff allocation
       b. class sizes assigned to each teacher
       c. grades or subjects taught by each teacher.
    2.   Read students' cumulative folders, noting kinds of comments made by specific teachers.
    3.   Check the textbook inventory and checkout system, noting:
       a. textbooks used by particular staff members
       b. reading levels of books used by specific teachers.
    4.   Observe teachers with students when possible, noting:
       a. common approaches taken with students
       b. reactions to student behavior
       c. types of materials and equipment used
       d. the interaction of students and teacher (motivational techniques, etc.) and non-verbal communication
       e. preferred classroom organization patterns of individual teachers.
    5.   Listen to teachers as they talk with students and with each other in the faculty room.
       a. Identify the school social structure.
       b. Note professional interaction.
       c. Note tones or voice and gestures used by specific teachers with students.
    6.   Talk with teachers directly.
       a. Identify their objectives.
       b. Identify their feelings and attitudes toward students, jobs, and co-workers.
       c. Identify types of instructional materials with which they feel most comfortable.
       d. Identify past use of the media center.
       e. Identify preferred instructional activities.
    7.   Talk with support personnel, identifying their special talents, abilities, and interests.
    8.   Read past media center reports, noting:
       a. past activities with specific teachers
       b. past use of media center and materials by specific teachers.

(Figure 13 is continued on page 76.)

Figure 13 (cont'd)

E. School Organization
    1.   Examine a chart of school system organization, noting:
        a. staff positions
        b. lines of authority.
    2.   Examine the school calendar.
        a. Identify school days.
        b. Identify special events, meetings, etc.
    3.   Talk with the principal.
        a. Identify the school organization.
        b. Note time allotments for subjects.
        c. Note teacher assignments and schedules.
    4.   Talk with grade level chairmen, individual teachers, etc., noting:
        a. time arrangements, schedules, etc.
        b. teacher groupings
        c. class sizes.

F. Curriculum
    1.   Examine the general school goals.
    2.   Examine a school program of studies or collection of curriculum documents.
        a. Determine subjects which are taught.
        b. Determine recommended amounts of time for subjects taught.
        c. Identify broad content areas.
        d. Identify skill areas.
    3.   Examine any written school objectives.
        a. Note plans for attaining these objectives.
        b. Identify how the media center is related to these objectives.
    4.   Examine written curriculum documents for each subject area.
        a. Note the content taught.
        b. Note any media skills which may already be identified in the documents.
    5.   Examine any sample units prepared by teachers in the school.
    6.   Examine the broad year's plans of teaching teams or individual teachers.
    7.   Examine state requirements and documents.

G. Teaching Methods and Approaches
    1.   Observe teachers teaching students.
    2.   Observe physical classroom arrangements.
    3.   Talk with teachers about preferred instructional activities and methods.
    4.   Listen to teachers when they discuss lessons, etc.

After developing a sequence of instructional objectives and preparing a school profile, the media specialist should be prepared to introduce the proposed media skills program to the school administration and teaching staff. This introduction may proceed in four stages:

Step One: Conference with the Principal

The media specialist should seek an initial conference with the school principal to discuss the proposed program. The general program rationale presented to the principal may closely follow the rationale in Chapter 1. If a media supervisor exists in the system, however, the principal may already have been given a general introduction to media skills instruction.

Discussion of the precise content and objectives of the program (see Chapter 2), instructional methods (see Chapter 3), and evaluation techniques (see Chapter 4) should be carefully related to the information gathered in the school profile. It is pointless to discuss the extensive use of learning centers, for example, if learning centers are seldom or never used by the teachers at the school. The program is far more likely to be endorsed and actively supported by the principal if it conforms to the realities of school life—that is, if the objectives are consistent with general school goals and objectives, if the suggested instructional methods are similiar to those preferred by the majority of the teachers at the school, and if the evaluation techniques are similiar to those in general use.

An important point which the media specialist must stress with the principal is that the proposed program is *not* a curriculum in the ordinary sense of that term. It is not a program to be taught by the media specialist alone; rather, it is most successful when integrated into everyday classroom instruction. Thorough integration will occur only with the full cooperation of the teaching staff, and such cooperation may be in large part a function of the endorsement and encouragement of the principal.

Step Two: Informal Conferences with Teachers

After obtaining initial support from the school principal, the media specialist may undertake a series of informal discussions with teachers. These discussions should be directed toward introducing and modifying the proposed sequence of media skills objectives to correspond with particular teaching methods and existing units of instruction. Teacher conferences may also include discussions of the integrated model of media skills instruction (see Chapter 1), teaching methods (see Chapter 3), and evaluation techniques (see Chapter 4).

Perhaps the most important concepts to be developed with teachers at this stage of implementation are the cooperative nature of media skills instruction, the joint instructional roles of teacher and media specialist, and the need to integrate media skills objectives into classroom instructional objectives.

Step Three: Demonstration Unit

The informal discussions indicated in Step Two should be held with *all* teachers. However, some teachers will naturally evince more initial interest than others. The media specialist may wish to undertake a demonstration unit in collaboration with one of these interested teachers, following the 13-step instructional model presented in Chapter 3. The unit, when completed with a class, serves the following important functions:

1.   It may be used in illustrating to other teachers the potential effectiveness of the proposed model of media skills instruction.

2. It may very well establish a valuable proselyte—the cooperating teacher—on the teaching staff.
3. It may indicate certain difficulties in the 13-step model imposed by particular local school conditions: e.g., limitations of school facilities, lack of staff planning time, etc. An approach to overcoming such difficulties may then be devised prior to full-scale implementation.

Step Four: Formal Faculty Discussions

Following the informal introduction of the proposed media skills program to the principal and teachers, the media specialist may plan a formal faculty meeting or series of meetings to finalize the initial implementation plan. This meeting or series of meetings should include:

1. An introduction and endorsement of the program by the principal and, if possible, the media supervisor.
2. A review of the major features of the classroom units to be taught at all grade levels, and the time sequence during which those units will be undertaken throughout the school year. A chart may then be prepared, outlining the teaching year at each grade level, as illustrated in Figure 14 (see page 80).

Once a chart of instructional units has been prepared, the media specialist may begin comparing the unit chart with the sequence of media skills objectives in order to determine which objectives might best be taught in connection with which units. Discussion with individual teachers may confirm the integration of particular media skills objectives into particular classroom units, and tentative plans may be made regarding methods of instruction, the respective instructional roles of teacher and media specialist, student groupings, and evaluation techniques. As the year progresses, each unit may be planned in detail, according to the 13-step instructional model presented in Chapter 3. As indicated in that model, careful attention must be paid to variables in the school environment, which will have been identified during the preparation of a school profile.

Obviously, a comprehensive program of media skills instruction cannot be introduced in one school year without seriously disrupting the on-going services of the media center, particularly if a system of regularly scheduled classes has previously been the accepted practice. Instead, introduction of the program may proceed according to the following schedule:

1. **Year One.** Introduction of the program at the administrative staff level by the media supervisor (according to the 7-step procedure presented above) and at the school level by the media specialist (according to the 4-step procedure presented above).

2. **Year Two.** Piloting of the program by the media specialist with one teacher and class.

3. **Year Three.** Maintain activities developed with pilot class in year two, and develop activities for one or two additional classes.

4.   **Years Four through Six.** Maintain previously developed activities, and
      develop activities for one or two additional classes each year.

The following series of daily schedules illustrate how a media skills program
might be introduced during years two through four without disrupting the on-going
services of a media center. In this particular example, the media center provided a
full range of services, including "library lessons," to scheduled classes (e.g., use
of dictionary, encyclopedia, reference materials, etc.), though these lessons were
entirely unrelated to classroom units. During year two, the media specialist worked
with the pilot second-grade teacher to plan and execute media skills activities
directly related to classroom units of instruction. During year three, another second
grade as well as the third grades were added to the pilot class. During year four,
fourth and fifth grades, and one sixth grade class were added. (See Figures 15, 16,
and 17 beginning on page 82.)

Figure 14: School Year's Plan

GRADE	September	October	November	December	January	February	March	April	May	June
Kindergarten										
Art	Care of Materials	Drawing	Painting	Paper	Sculpture	Ceramics		Stitchery and Weaving		
Careers	Awareness of School Personnel									
English/Reading	(Reading Readiness Program)									
Health/Safety	Safety on the Way to School		Breakfast		Clothing for Good Health					
Math	(Conceptual at appropriate levels)									
Music	Singing and Rhythms				Rhythms					
Phys. Ed.	Basic Movements (hopping, skipping, etc.)					Rope Jumping		Parachute Play		Ball Tossing
Science		Weather changes			Magnets		Animal Life		Land and Water Plants	
Social Studies	"Myself"	Holidays and Seasons (as they occur)								
Grade One										
Art	Care of Materials	Drawing	Painting	Paper	Sculpture	Ceramics		Stitchery and Weaving		
Careers		Careers of Our Parents and Those We Know								
English/Reading	(Basal Readers)									
Health/Safety	Safety at School		Safety at Home	Food for Health	Dental Health		Posture			
Math	(Conceptual at appropriate levels)									
Music	Singing and Rhythms				Appreciation	Creative Dance and Rhythm				
Phys. Ed.	Basic Movements		Climbing Time		Ball Playing				Team Games	
Science	Forms of Energy	Seasons		Weather	Forms of Life	Forms of Matter		Seeds	Plants in Spring	
Social Studies	Responsibility in School	"My Family"			Homes	My Neighborhood		Community Market		
Grade Two										
Art	Care of Materials	Drawing	Painting	Paper	Sculpture	Ceramics		Stitchery and Weaving		
Careers		Jobs of the People in My Community								
English/Reading	(Basal Readers and Language Experience)									
Health/Safety	Safety at School		Food for Health		Teeth and Eating Habits			Fire and Home Safety		
Math	(Conceptual at appropriate levels)									
Music	Singing and Rhythms	Rhythms			Appreciation (Mood, Melody, etc.)		Creative Movement			
Phys. Ed.	Basic Movements		Group Sports		Rope Jumping					
Science		Life Cycles	Plants		Energy	Light	Fossils	Seasons (Earth, Moon, and Sun)		
Social Studies	School	Neighborhood	Community Helpers		Cities and Towns		Communication	Transportation		

Figure 14 (cont'd)

GRADE	September	October	November	December	January	February	March	April	May	June
Grade Three										
Art	Care of Materials	Drawing	Painting	Paper	Sculpture		Ceramics		Stitchery and Weaving	
Careers	Careers of People in Other Lands									
English/Reading		Folklore	Fables	Mythology	Nonsense	Fairy Tales	Human Relations			Adventure
Health/Safety	School Safety	Fire Safety		Home Safety	Dental Health		Disease		Bicycle Safety	
Math	(Conceptual at appropriate levels)									
Music	Group Singing		Rhythm	Listening	Melody, Harmony, Rhythm			Making Instruments		
Phys. Ed.	Team Games	(Ball Games)			Tumbling		Physical Fitness		Ball Games	
Science	Sun and Energy	Matter			Plants and Seeds					
Social Studies	Navahos	Arab Village	Animal Habitats	Mexico	Eskimos	Japan		Populations Washington, D.C.		Africa
Grade Four										
Art	Care of Materials	Drawing	Painting	Paper	Sculpture	Ceramics			Stitchery and Weaving	
Careers	Careers of Americans through the Ages									
English/Reading	(Individualized Reading Program)									
Health/Safety	School Safety	Fire Safety		Home Safety	Human Body		Nutrition		Bicycle Safety	
Math	(Conceptual at appropriate levels)									
Music	Group Singing		Rhythm	Listening		Making and Playing Instruments			Reading Music	
Phys. Ed.	Team Games					Tumbling	Physical Fitness		Ball Games	
Science	Heat	Sound	Light	Environmental Change	Chemical Change		Life Cycles		Classification of Life	
Social Studies	U.S. Exploration		Colonial Life	American Revolution		Early Exploration	Westward Movement			Civil War
Grade Five										
Art	Care of Materials	Drawing	Painting	Paper	Sculpture	Ceramics			Stitchery and Weaving	
Careers	Careers in U.S. Geographical Regions									
English/Reading	Poetry		Fantasy		Mystery		Fables		Values in Literature	
Health/Safety	School Safety	Fire Safety		Family Life			Nutrition			
Math	(Conceptual at appropriate levels)									
Music	Group Singing		Instruments	Folk Dance	Reading Music	Melody	Harmony	Rhythm	Form	
Phys. Ed.	Team Games and Fitness				Basketball		Soccer	Softball		
Science	Machines	Matter and Energy			Adaptation of Living Things		Geologic Changes		Oceanography	
Social Studies	Alaska and Hawaii	Pacific Northwest		Dry Southwest	Plains and Prairies		Dry West	The South	Northeast	
Grade Six										
Art	Care of Materials	Drawing	Painting	Paper	Sculpture		Ceramics		Stitchery and Weaving	
Careers	Careers in Ancient Cultures									
English/Reading	Humor		Man and Nature		Man Living with Others		Point of View			
Health/Safety	School Safety	Fire Safety			Smoking		Drugs and Stimulants			
Music	Singing in Harmony		Instruments	Square Dance	Reading Music		Instruments and the Orchestra		Opera	Ballet
Phys. Ed.	Team Games					Rope Climbing	Soccer		Softball	
Science	Energy, Force, and Motion		Physical Change		Green Plants and Energy		Cells	Geologic Changes		Solar System
Social Studies	Mesopotamia	Egypt	Greece		Rome		Feudalism		Renaissance	

Figure 15: Year Two (Sample Week during the Middle of the Year)

	M	T	W	T	F
8:30–9:00	(With the aide, the media specialist provides equipment, books, etc. for teachers. Students check out materials before classes start. Brief informal talks with teachers occur regarding materials selection, class projects, specific students, orders, requests, etc.)				
9:00–9:20	Classes in homeroom; media specialist prepares for day's activities; media center is always available for check out of materials.				
9:20–10:15	6th grade class from Reading/Language Arts (scheduled for reference tools lesson)	Prepare bibliography for 5th grade unit	5th grade class from Reading/Language Arts (scheduled encyclopedia lesson)	6th grade class from Reading/Language Arts (scheduled for reference tools lesson)	5th grade class from Reading/Language Arts (scheduled for encyclopedia lesson)
10:15–10:45	3rd grade class during their math class (scheduled class)	3rd grade class during their math class (scheduled class)	4th grade class during math (card catalog lesson)	4th grade class during math (card catalog lesson)	Work on book order and selection
10:45–11:15	Kindergarten Story Time	2nd grade class (scheduled class)	Work on monthly report to be sent to media supervisor	Gather material for 6th grade teacher	
11:15–12:00	File cards in catalog	Review card catalog project with aide	Grade papers from 6th and 3rd grade classes	Prepare transparency for 4th grade teacher	Plan with 2nd grade pilot teacher
12:00–12:30	Lunch	Lunch	Lunch	Lunch	Lunch
12:30–1:00	Kindergarten Story Time	Pilot 2nd grade works on media center activity with Social Studies emphasis (transportation activity) connected with their unit		Give in-service to volunteers on book repair and filmstrip repair	Meet with principal to discuss new video tape equipment
1:00–1:30	1st Grade Class Story Time				Prepare book display for holiday
1:30–2:00	1st Grade Class Story Time		Work with music teacher to select records for purchase		Meet with aide to plan for next week's activities
2:00–2:45	Media Center open to 5th and 6th grades for Social Studies class work	Media Center open to 5th and 6th grades for Social Studies class work	Media Center open to 5th and 6th grades for Social Studies class work	Media Center open to 5th and 6th grades for Social Studies class work	Media Center open to 5th and 6th grades for Social Studies class work
2:45–3:15	Collect materials and equipment requests from teachers				
3:15–4:00	Faculty meeting	Work on equipment inventory	Gather material for holiday reading	Gather material for holiday reading	Organize materials for next week

Figure 16: Year Three (Sample Week during the Middle of the Year)

	M	T	W	T	F
8:30–9:00	(With the aide, the media specialist provides equipment, books, etc., for teachers. Students check out materials before classes start. Brief informal talks with teachers occur regarding materials selection, class projects, specific students, orders, requests, etc.)				
9:00–9:20	Classes in homeroom; media specialist sets up for day's activities.				
9:20–10:00	6th grade class from Reading/Language Arts (scheduled class)	6th grade class from Reading/Language Arts (scheduled class)	Work with alphabetizing skills with small groups of 2nd graders from both classes (related to the reading program)—Pilot group		Videotapes the Speech teacher
10:00–10:45	5th grade class from Reading/Language Arts (scheduled class)	5th grade class from Reading/Language Arts (scheduled class)			
10:45–11:15	Plan with pilot 3rd grade teachers during their Art and Phys. Ed.	Kindergarten Story Time	4th grade class from Math (scheduled class)	4th grade class from Math (scheduled class)	Work on inventory problems
11:15–12:00	Work on acquisition of new materials with aide	Collect 6th grade unit materials	Work on fairy tale bibliography	Videotape music lesson with music teacher	
12:00–12:30	Lunch	Lunch	Lunch	Lunch	Lunch
12:30–1:00	1st grade class Story Time	Kindergarten Story Time	1st grade class Story Time	Collect I-Can-Read materials for 1st grade classes	Continue to work on inventory
1:00–2:00	Pilot 3rd grade classes work on Social Studies projects. Small groups use the card catalog and book indexes to find information for clothing unit.				
2:00–3:00	Open media center work for 5th and 6th grade classes				
3:00–3:15	Collect equipment and clean-up				
3:15–4:00	Faculty Meeting	Confer with 2nd grade teachers	Confer with 3rd grade teachers on progress of groups	Plan with 5th grade teacher	Review and plan work schedule with aide

Figure 17: Year Four (Sample Week during the Middle of the Year)

	M	T	W	T	F
8:30–9:00	(With the aide, the media specialist provides equipment, books, etc., for teachers. Students check out materials before classes start. Brief informal talks with teachers occur regarding materials selection, class projects, specific students, orders, requests, etc.)				
9:00–9:20	Videotaped exercise shown to classes while students in homeroom	Prepare for the day			Videotape new show while students in home-room
9:20–10:00	6th grade class (scheduled class)	3rd grade class work on indexing skills for reading in four small groups			Work on book order and selection of materials for purchase
10:00–10:45	Work on preparation of slide/tape script for a P.T.A. program			Work with the Phys. Ed. teacher to weed record collection	
10:45–11:15	Kindergarten Story Time	1st grade class Story Time	Meet with gifted 5th grade reading club group	2nd grade class in three groups for Math related story time (geometry)	Gather materials for 2nd grade unit
11:15–12:00	4th graders work on dictionary learning centers in small groups (from reading)				
12:00–12:30	Lunch	Lunch	Lunch	Lunch	Lunch
12:30–1:00	Kindergarten Story Time	1st grade class Story Time	Work with parent volunteers to start print inventory	Give special book talk to 3rd grade class	Give special book talk to 3rd grade class
1:00–1:45	5th grade class introduction to outlining for science project	Work with 5th grade students on projects related to science	Work with 5th grade students on outlines for class	Work with 6th grade class on preparation of videotape of science experiments in small groups	Plan with 2nd grade teacher
1:45–2:30	5th grade class introduction to outlining for science project	Set up book display on winter sports	Work on plans for a special book reading contest		Meet with 4th grade group to gather materials for a Social Studies play
3:00–3:15	Collect equipment and clean up				
3:15–4:00	Faculty Meeting	Meet with 3rd grade teachers	Meet with the principal for P.T.A. meeting	Review lessons with 3rd grade teachers	Review weekly plans with aide

ILLUSTRATIVE UNITS

The sample instructional units which follow are those which might have been prepared and taught by the media specialist and the pilot second-grade teacher during year two. Each unit indicates the time of year that the unit might be taught, the classroom instructional unit into which media skills objectives are integrated, the media skills objectives (referred to the sequence of objectives, Chapter 2) of the unit, student groupings, activities, and assessments.

Unit I: Safety and School (Social Studies)

Time: Late September

Instructional Unit: Safety and School (Social Studies)

Media Skills Objectives: Find specific information using picture clues in decoding (review of grade K-1 objective).

Student Grouping: Entire class

Activity: Students will prepare a large mural or bulletin board entitled "Safety in the Media Center." Pictures may be cut from magazines and vendors' catalogs illustrating safe use of instructional equipment, use of stools to obtain books from upper shelves, etc.

Assessment: Each student will locate one appropriate picture, cut it out, and mount it on the bulletin board.

Unit II: Alphabetizing and Picture Dictionaries
(Reading and Language Arts)

Time: October through November

Instructional Unit: Alphabetizing and Picture Dictionaries (Reading and Language Arts)

Media Skills Objectives:
1. Locate specific picture or easy books using the author's last name (review of grade K-1 objective).
2. Select a picture dictionary in order to match words with pictures (review of grade K-1 objective).
3. Use a picture dictionary (review of grade K-1 objective).
4. Alphabetize by the first letter in a word or first letter in an author's last name (review of grade K-1 objective).
5. Alphabetize to the second letter of a word or author's last name.
6. Alphabetize to the third letter of a word or an author's last name (grade 3 objective, only for appropriate groups).
7. Find words in a dictionary (grade 3 objective, only for appropriate groups).

Unit II (cont'd)

Student Grouping: Some activities for the entire class, some for small groups (divided into six reading groups since diagnosis indicated that alphabetizing and dictionary skills correlated with reading level).

Activities:

Activity One (entire class): After a brief discussion of the alphabet, students will be told that they will practice the alphabet. A clothesline will be stretched across the room and each letter of the alphabet will be attached to the line using clothespins, leaving some space between each letter. Students will be divided into two groups, and each student will be given a picture of a particular word with that word written on the picture. Students will be asked to attach their picture words to the clothesline in proper alphabetical position. The group finishing first in a relay race to put their words in the correct place, wins the game.

Assessment: Each student will attach one picture-word to the clothesline in the appropriate alphabetical position.

Activity Two (only the two lowest groups in reading achievement): On a bulletin board, large letters representing the entire alphabet will be displayed in alphabetical order. Students will be asked to look through magazines to find pictures which illustrate "feeling words" for each letter of the alphabet (e.g., A-angry; S-silly, sad; etc.). Pictures will be cut out and attached to the bulletin board beside the appropriate letter.

Assessment: Each student will locate and cut out an appropriate picture and place it on the bulletin board beside the proper letter of the alphabet.

Activity Three (all groups): Five areas will be set up in the media center, with one area assigned to each of the five senses. Each area will be provided with word cards related to that particular sense (e.g., touch area: warm, soft, hard, rough, smooth, scratchy, cold, etc.). Words should be chosen in such a way that some areas require only one-letter alphabetizing (all words in an area begin with a different letter), some require two-letter alphabetizing (some words begin with the same letter), and some require three-letter alphabetizing. Since pre-testing indicated that alphabetizing ability corresponded with the reading level, higher achieving reading groups will be assigned to two- and three-letter alphabetizing areas and lower achieving reading groups will be assigned to one-letter alphabetizing areas. An initial explanation of "sense words" will be given and groups will then be told to alphabetize the cards in their area.

Assessment: Student groups will correctly alphabetize the sense word cards in assigned areas.

Activity Four (entire class): Students will be shown the location of easy and picture books, and the nature of these books will be explained (e.g., "These are special books because of their pictures. We may read them by looking at the pictures." etc.). It will be pointed out that each book has a "home" and an "address" in the media center. The "home" of the book is that section of shelves labeled with the same letter as the "address" on the spine of the

Unit II (cont'd)

Activities (cont'd):

book. Students will be told that they may select a book from a particular "home" (e.g., "D Home" or "W Home").

Assessment: Each student will select a book from the designated "home."

Activity Five (all groups—the two higher-achieving groups may proceed to this activity directly after Activity Four; lower-achieving groups may undertake the activity on another day): The "homes" and "addresses" of books will be reviewed. A worksheet (see Figure 18) will be given to students and they will be asked to cut out the "book" and place it in its proper "home" on the worksheet. Subsequently, each student will be given one cut-out "book," they will be lined up and when told to "go" will find the "home" of their cut-out on the media center shelves. The student finding the correct "home" first wins the game. The game may be repeated several times.

Figure 18

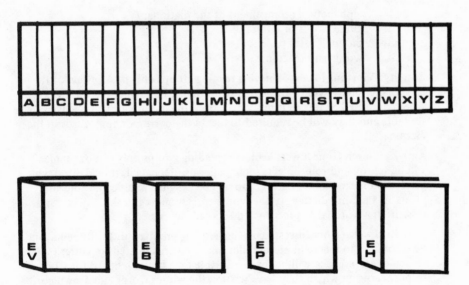

Put the books in the correct "homes."

Assessment: Students will place cut-outs in appropriate "homes" on the worksheet. Students will locate the proper "home" on the media center shelves for a cut-out given to them.

Activity Six (lower-achieving reading groups only): Arrangement of easy books will be reviewed, and a relay race will be arranged in which two teams will be given a number of paper book cut-outs and asked to place the cut-outs in the proper "home" on the shelves in relay fashion. The team that first shelves all cut-outs correctly wins.

Unit II (cont'd)

Activities (cont'd)

Assessment: Students will correctly shelve all paper cut-outs.

Activity Seven (all groups): Each student will be given a small stack of easy books and told to shelve them.

Assessment: The media specialist will observe students to see that each student shelves the books correctly.

Activity Eight (four lowest-achieving groups only): Familiar objects that may be found in a picture dictionary will be placed on a table. The items will be discussed and students will identify them. Then students will be asked how they might find the written word representing the items. Picture dictionaries will be introduced and, with the help of the media specialist, students will be asked to locate each of the items in the dictionary.

Activity Nine (four lowest-achieving reading groups only): Using the same objects and picture dictionary as indicated in Activity Eight, students will be introduced to:
1.   alphabetical arrangement of the dictionary
2.   guide words or letters
3.   pictures
4.   words and meanings

Activity Ten (four lowest-achieving reading groups only): A review of the picture dictionary will be presented to students. Following the review, a worksheet comprised of ten pictures copied from the dictionary will be given to students and they will be required to locate the corresponding words in the dictionary.

Activity Eleven (four lowest-achieving reading groups only): Four tables will be set up, and four objects (e.g., ball, scissors, pencil, thread, etc.) will be placed on each table. Each group will be assigned a table and told to locate in a picture dictionary the words corresponding to the objects, and to write the words that precede and succeed the correct word.

Activity Twelve (four lowest-achieving reading groups only): Students will be instructed to locate in picture dictionaries words related to winter (snow, ice, cold, etc.). Space will be made available on a bulletin board for students to post cards on which they have written the winter words and drawn corresponding pictures. When all cards have been posted, students will be asked to rearrange them in alphabetical order.

Assessment (Activities Eight through Twelve): Given three objects, each student will locate those objects in a picture dictionary.

Activity Thirteen (two highest-achieving reading groups only): The classroom teacher will work with the upper two groups on alphabetizing and dictionary skills using lecture, demonstration, and discussion techniques while the media specialist works with the lower-achieving groups on activities eight through twelve.

Unit III: Creative Dramatics (Physical Education)

Time: Early December

Instructional Unit: Creative Dramatics (Physical Education)

Media Skills Objective: Identify and describe an auditory sequence of events.

Student Grouping: Entire class

Activity: Students will be told the story of the *Gingerbread Man*. The media specialist will discuss the story with students and ask them to describe what happened to each person who wanted to catch the gingerbread man. Each student will receive a gingerbread man to eat. Certain students then will be asked to enact the story in proper sequence with small props, as other students retell the story.

Assessment: Students asked to enact the story will accurately portray the series of actions in proper sequence. Students asked to retell the story will accurately describe the enacted events.

Unit IV: Geometric Shapes (Mathematics)

Time: Middle of January

Instructional Unit: Geometric Shapes (Mathematics)

Media Skills Objectives:
1. Use color (hue, value, intensity), line, and shape to produce a picture based on ideas in a story or reading (review of grade K-1 objective).
2. Use a chosen method involving lines, shapes, colors, and textures to express ideas, feelings, or experiences obtained from a resource.

Student Grouping: Entire class

Activity: After the telling of Gerald McDermot's Indian story, *Arrow to the Sun*, students will be asked to produce a picture based on the story. Since the illustrations in the book are geometric in design, patterns of squares, circles, rectangles, triangles, etc., will be given to the students. They will be instructed to use the patterns to cut out shapes from construction paper, and to assemble the shapes into a picture representing a scene from the story. When pasted and completed, the pictures may be displayed in proper sequence.

Assessment: Using cut geometric patterns, each student will produce a picture based on the mood or action in Gerald McDermot's *Arrow to the Sun.*

Unit V: Cities and City Life (Social Studies)

Time: End of January

Instructional Unit: Cities and City Life (Social Studies)

Media Skills Objective: Identify and trace the development of a plot.

Unit V (cont'd)

Activity: After hearing the story of *The Little House* by Virginia Lee Burton, students will be asked to discuss the growth and development of cities through a description of the plot of the story and the historical changes in the little house.

Assessment: Each student will contribute to the discussion of city growth in relation to the plot of Virginia Lee Burton's *The Little House.*

Unit VI: Authors and Illustrators (Language Arts and Art)

Time: February through March

Instructional Unit: Authors and Illustrators (Language Arts and Art)

Media Skills Objectives:
1. Identify and describe:
    a. a written sequence of events
    b. a pictorial sequence of events
    c. an audio sequence of events
    d. the main idea in diverse media materials
    e. visual images using line, color, and shape (review of grade K-1 objectives)
2. Identify and trace:
    a. the development of a character (motivation)
    b. the setting of a story
3. Identify fantasy, unreality, impossibility, and incongruity in a resource.
4. Predict the outcome of a narrative.

Student Grouping: Entire class

Activities:

Activity One: After a review of authors and stories with which they are familiar, students will be told the story of *Madeline* by Ludwig Bemelmans. Background information about the author will be given, and students will be asked to discuss what the author said about different kinds of schools and about operations and hospitals (setting).

Assessment: Each student will participate in the discussion.

Activity Two: After a review of authorship, students will be told *Where the Wild Things Are* by Maurice Sendak. After the story, students will be asked to decide if the story is real, fantasy, or make-believe and to identify what really might have happened. Background information may be given about Sendak (e.g., he drew the "wild things" from people he knew). Students will be asked to sit or act like a "wild thing" without touching anyone or making a sound and later to draw a picture of the "wild thing" they enact.

Assessment: Each student will participate in the discussion, act like a "wild thing," and draw a "wild thing."

Unit VI (cont'd)

Activities (cont'd)

Activity Three: Background information on Ezra Jack Keats will be given and *The Snowy Day* told to students. If available, the 16mm film or the sound filmstrip by Weston Woods will be shown. The word-collage and other illustrations will be discussed.

Assessment: Each student will participate in the discussion.

Activity Four: Students will be given crayons and paper, and an audio-tape, prepared by the media specialist, telling the story of *Andy and the Lion* by James Daugherty. As students listen to the tape, they will be asked to draw illustrations related to the taped story. After hearing the story and completing their illustrations, students will be shown the actual book and illustrations and will be asked to compare the real illustrations with their own.

Assessment: Each student will produce an illustration based on an audio-tape of Daugherty's *Andy and the Lion* and will participate in an oral comparison of his illustration with Daugherty's.

Activity Five: After a review of background information on Ezra Jack Keats, a brief discussion will be held with students concerning their own brothers and sisters and then they will be told the story of *Peter's Chair*. In subsequent discussions, students will be asked questions like:
1. What were Peter's feelings and what made him act as he did?
2. What happened in the story?
3. Was there anything funny in the story?
4. Was Peter jealous?
5. Have you ever been jealous?
6. Have you ever seen other books by this author?

Assessment: Each student will participate in the discussion. (Other activities may be added as time and scheduling allow.)

Unit Assessment: When asked the question "What does an author do?", each student will orally describe what an author does, including references to setting, plot, and character.

Unit VII: Transportation (Social Studies)

Time: April

Instructional Unit: Transportation (Social Studies)

Media Skills Objectives:
1. Review of Unit II objectives (two lowest-achieving reading groups only).
2. Find specific information using visuals (pictures, charts, filmstrips, etc.) and listening to audio materials (review of grade K-1 objective).
3. Identify a fact, truth, reality, or possibility in a resource.
4. Distinguish between fact and fiction.
5. Make a simple graph.

Unit VII (cont'd)

Student Grouping: Entire class, six reading groups

Activities:

Activity One (two lowest reading groups): Since students in the two lowest-achieving reading groups are still having some difficulty with alphabetizing, a tape of transportation sounds will be prepared and played for these students. A worksheet will be given to students which lists paired transportation vehicles and pictures of those vehicles (see Figure 19).

Figure 19

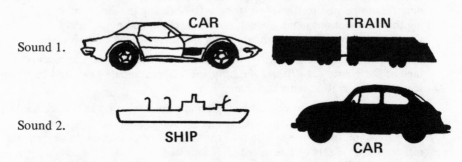

Students will be asked to circle the word representing the vehicle that produced each sound, and then to write the circled words in alphabetical order. (This is preparation for indexing skills.)

Assessment: Students will complete the identification/alphabetizing worksheet with no errors.

Activity Two (entire class): After some introductory information on the author, students will be told the story of *Little Toot* by Hardie Gramatky. In subsequent discussion, students will be asked to compare the tugboats in the story with real boats and tugboats and to identify which parts of the story are real and which are not.

Assessment: Each student will participate in the discussion.

Activity Three (entire class in groups): Short paragraphs regarding various modes of transportation will be located in books and typed on 3x5-inch cards. Small pictures of those modes of transportation will be pasted on a separate set of cards. Students will be asked to match paragraph cards and picture cards.

Assessment: Students will correctly match all paragraph and picture cards.

Activity Four (entire class): A poll will be taken of the types of transportation students have used. Students will be asked to prepare a simple graph of the resulting data.

Assessment: Each student will prepare a simple graph of the data obtained in the transportation poll.

Unit VII (cont'd)

Activities (cont'd)

Activity Five (entire class in groups): An audio tape will be prepared which consists of a series of descriptive sequences about modes of transportation. In each sequence, an incorrect or untrue statement will be included. Students will be asked to identify the incorrect or untrue statements.

Assessment: Students will identify all incorrect or untrue statements in the audio tape.

Activity Six (entire class): Students will examine several modes of transportation (wagons, sailboats, steamships, automobiles, etc.) through filmstrips, pictures, and books. Four problems will be given to the students. Such problems might include transporting several baskets of apples from an orchard to a barn over a bumpy road. The students, using knowledge gained from materials, will determine the following for each problem:

> the most comfortable form of transportation
> the fastest form of transportation
> the slowest form of transportation
> the most expensive form of transportation
> the safest form of transportation

Assessment: The student will correctly complete at least two of the problems.

Unit VIII: Seasons (Science)

Time: May

Instructional Unit: Seasons (Science)

Media Skills Objectives:
1. Translate oral or written directions from a resource into a product or action (review of grade K-1 objective).
2. Record information on a cassette tape recorder (review of grade K-1 objective).
3. Illustrate a story or reading by making a series of pictures, clay figures, creative movements, etc.

Student Grouping: Entire class

Activity: Several poems about Spring will be read to students. Following the reading, students will be asked to discuss how Spring makes them feel, and music evoking Spring will be played. Students will then be asked to gather small natural materials that indicate the coming of Spring, such as tiny leaves, flowers, insects, etc. Students will be given a demonstration on making handmade slides, and will prepare slides using gathered natural materials. Such slides may be prepared by placing tiny natural materials on clear acetate film cut to proper size, covering the acetate and materials with laminating film, sealing the slide with a tacking iron and mounting the sealed acetate in

Unit VIII (cont'd)

Activity (cont'd)

a slide mount. When slides have been completed, students will be asked to arrange and project them as the "Spring music" is played.

Assessment: Each student will prepare a "Spring slide" and will cooperate with other students in projecting the slides as "Spring music" is played.

CONCLUSION

The foregoing list of media skills units is only a very brief indication of major activities undertaken in one year by a media specialist in connection with one pilot second-grade teacher and class. In a fully operating media skills program, introduced over a four- or five-year period, similar units are planned and executed with *all* teachers and classes. Problems involving planning and preparation time, scheduling, diagnosis and assessment of students, and the reconciliation of all the variables of instructional methodology are complex and time-consuming. It may well require even longer than the four or five years indicated in the example to develop a consistent and comprehensive program. We do not suggest that the development of such a program is easy. We do suggest that it is possible, following a rational instructional method, and that it is worth the required effort.

SUMMARY

There are several identifiable elements in any plan for the implementation of a media skills program. If a system-level supervisory staff exists for media centers or school libraries, that staff may develop a sequence of media skills objectives applicable to all schools within the system and an in-service program designed to introduce media specialists and administrators to the proposed program of media skills instruction. Media specialists may, in turn, introduce the sequence of objectives and the integrated instructional model to the school principal and teaching staff with the support of the media supervisor. Steps in this introductory process may include:

1. the preparation of a school profile
2. conferences with the principal
3. informal conferences with teachers
4. the preparation of a demonstration unit
5. formal faculty discussions.

Following this introduction, a year's instructional plan may be developed, and implementation may commence.

PART II–SAMPLE MEDIA SKILLS ACTIVITIES

INTRODUCTION

The sample activities contained in Part II are designed to illustrate the range of media skills activities that can be integrated into classroom units of instruction. Since the recommended model of media skills instruction presented in Part I of this book requires that media skills activities be integrated into classroom units, each sample activity is headed with the title of a possible classroom unit into which that activity might be integrated. The units and headings were specifically selected owing to their frequent appearance in curriculum documents from all parts of the country.

In addition to specifying a possible classroom unit into which each activity might be integrated, each activity contains the appropriate media skills objectives, performance objectives, student levels, learning strategies (teaching methods), necessary resources, learning activities, and assessment criteria.

The activities in Part II are not to be regarded in any way as a consistent or systematic "curriculum" for media skills instruction. They are designed only as samples, illustrating the widest possible range of objectives, student levels, learning strategies, activities, and assessment techniques. It is recommended that they be used as models for the design of activities appropriate to local curricula and media skills objectives, rather than as ready-made lesson plans.

ACTIVITIES

Art—Drawing

Media Skills Objective: Use color (hue, value, and intensity), line, and shape to produce a picture based on ideas in a story or reading.

Level: 2-5

Learning Strategy: Learning center

Performance Objective: Given a selection of seven centers describing kinds of illustrations, the student will select three and prepare a picture about the story at each center using the style of illustrator of that story.

Resources: Seven Caldecott-winning books, tempera paints, watercolor paints, pencils, pastels or chalk, crayons, colored bits of paper for collages, paper, and professional books such as *Caldecott Medal Books: 1938-1957*, edited by Bertha M. Miller and Elinor W. Field, or *Caldecott Medal Books: 1956-1965*, edited by Lee Kingman.

Activity: Seven Caldecott-winning books will be selected. An explanation of how the author drew his pictures will be developed into a learning center. Picture directions or taped directions may be made for students to follow at each area. Students will be told that these books are award-winning books because of their illustrations. Students will look at the book and listen to or read about the process the author used to make his particular illustrations. Then, the students will make a picture in the same style.

Example:

Figure 20

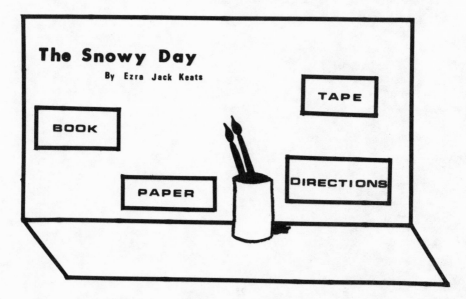

Art—Drawing (cont'd)

Activity (cont'd)

The Snowy Day was illustrated using collage. The author and illustrator made the bed linen from a piece of Belgian canvas. The mother's dress was made from a piece of oilcloth.

Directions for collage:
1. When you have an idea for your picture, decide where you want the figures in your picture to go on the paper.
2. Think about the picture and how you would like people to feel when they see it.
3. Decide on the colors you would like to have in the picture.
4. Select pieces of paper, cloth, or other materials which you want on the paper.
5. You may paint a background or use collage.
6. You may cut pieces to make the figures for your collage.
7. Put the pieces on the background.
8. When the pieces are in the correct place, glue them to the background.
9. Paint parts of the collage pieces if you wish.

Other books that might be used include:
The Big Snow by Berta and Elmer Hader
The Biggest Bear by Lynd Ward
The Little House by Virginia Lee Burton
Time of Wonder by Robert McCloskey
A Tree Is Nice by Janice May Udry
Where the Wild Things Are by Maurice Sendak

Assessment Criteria: The student will complete a picture about the assigned book in the same style as the original illustrator.

■ ■ ■

Career Education

Media Skills Objective: Use a telephone directory

Level: 3

Learning Strategy: Lecture; drill

Performance Objective: Given a list of careers, the student will find people with a last name identical with the listed careers and give the telephone number of those people.

Resources: Telephone directory, career name worksheet, and pencil.

Activity: The teacher will first discuss the idea that people were often named for their jobs. When the teacher has explained the use of the telephone directory for finding telephone numbers, the students will be given an activity. Students will see how many of these names they can find in the telephone directory

Career Education (cont'd)

Activity (cont'd)

within a given time (30 minutes). They will list the number by the name when it has been found.

Career Name Worksheet:

Abbot	Cutter	Judge	Queen
Baker	Dancer	King	Racer
Archer	Dean	Lawyer	Reader
Armer	Dentist	Leatherman	Rector
Banker	Designer	Lockerman	Rider
Barber	Dinerman	Lord	Sailor
Barker	Diver	Maison	Sargent
Baron	Doctor	Major	Sellers
Bishop	Drummer	Marshall	Settler
Boatman	Driver	Mayor	Shepherd
Bookbinder	Duke	Merchant	Sheriff
Bowler	Dyer	Middleman	Shipper
Bowman	Falconer	Miller	Shoemaker
Brakeman	Farmer	Milkman	Singer
Brewer	Fiddler	Miner	Skinner
Bridgeman	Fireman	Monk	Sowers
Butcher	Fisher	Nanny	Spinner
Butler	Forrester	Packer	Squire
Buyer	Gambler	Parker	Stockman
Caddy	Gardener	Parson	Surgeon
Camper	Glassman	Partner	Tailor
Carpenter	Goldsmith	Pastor	Tester
Carstarter	Groom	Potter	Trainer
Champion	Hammerer	Powdermaker	Trimmer
Cheeseman	Healer	Pressman	Weaver
Clayman	Hunter	Prince	Woodman
Cook	Jeweler	Printer	Workman
Couchman	Joiner	Quarterman	Writer

Assessment Criteria: The student will complete the activity according to a specified criterion (e.g., ten telephone numbers in 30 minutes). Variations of this exercise include lists of animals, geographic terms, places, things, etc.

■ ■ ■

Health

Media Skills Objective: Find words in a dictionary

Level: 4

Learning Strategy: Game

Performance Objective: Given words related to the human body to find in a dictionary, the student will locate the words in order to play a game.

Health (cont'd)

Resources: Game and dictionary

Activity: Prepare a game which students will play, four at a time. The object of the game is to move the players along a marked path on a model of a particular part of the body such as the ear (Figure 21). The first player through is the winner. To move players, the participant spins a spinner. This tells how many spaces may be moved. The participant draws a card and uses a dictionary to answer the question on the card. The questions deal with terminology related to the ear or other chosen body part.

Figure 21

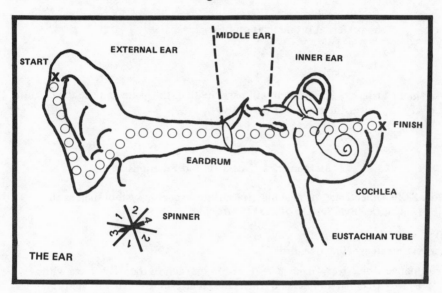

Sample:

    1.   How many syllables in the words "inner ear"?

Answer: Three

Questions should deal with spelling, pronunciation, syllabication, parts of speech, and meaning. Students, after looking for the word in the dictionary and answering the question, may check their answer by looking at the back of the card. The student will then move the player according to the spinner. If the student's answer is incorrect, no move may be made. If a player lands on an occupied space, the player occupying that space must move back one space.

Health (cont'd)

Activity (cont'd)
> Sample Questions:
>> The word cochlea is:
>>> a. an adverb
>>> *b. a noun
>>> c. an adjective
>>> d. a verb
>>
>> The word which means, "a spiral-shaped cavity of the inner ear" is:
>>> a. eustachian tube
>>> b. stirrup
>>> c. anvil
>>> *d. cochlea
>>
>> The preferred pronunciation of cochlea is:
>>> *a. kok' lē ə
>>> b. cok lĕ' ă
>>> c. kōk lē ə'

Assessment Criteria: The student will participate in the game and use the dictionary to answer the questions correctly.

■   ■   ■

Mathematics—Decimals and Fractions

Media Skills Objective: Arrange materials using a specific system such as the *Dewey Decimal System of Classification.*

Level: 5

Learning Strategy: Practice, drill

Performance Objective: Given a set of books on each of the fifty states with Dewey Decimal numbers on the spine labels, the student will identify the number and the proper place of each book when arranged in sequence.

Resources: Set of books on each of the fifty states, worksheet, and pencil.

Activity: The teacher will set up an area where the fifty state books may be placed. The students will be given a worksheet.

917.41	Maine	917.69	Kentucky
917.42	New Hampshire	917.71	Ohio
917.43	Vermont	917.72	Indiana
917.44	Massachusetts	917.73	Illinois
917.45	Rhode Island	917.74	Michigan
917.46	Connecticut	917.75	Wisconsin
917.47	New York	917.76	Minnesota
917.48	Pennsylvania	917.77	Iowa
917.49	New Jersey	917.78	Missouri
917.51	Delaware	917.81	Kansas
917.52	Maryland	917.82	Nebraska

(Listing continued on next page.)

Mathematics—Decimals and Fractions (cont'd)

Activity (cont'd)

917.53	District of Columbia	917.83	South Dakota
917.54	West Virginia	917.84	North Dakota
917.55	Virginia	917.86	Montana
917.56	North Carolina	917.87	Wyoming
917.57	South Carolina	917.88	Colorado
917.58	Georgia	917.89	New Mexico
917.59	Florida	917.91	Arizona
917.61	Alabama	917.92	Utah
917.62	Mississippi	917.93	Nevada
917.63	Louisiana	917.94	California
917.64	Texas	917.95	Oregon
917.66	Oklahoma	917.96	Idaho
917.67	Arkansas	917.97	Washington
917.68	Tennessee	917.98	Alaska
		919.69	Hawaii

Worksheet:

1. Utah is represented by what number? Is this number more or less than Indiana's?
2. Colorado is represented by what number? Is this number more or less than Iowa's?
3. When these books are arranged in order on the shelf, they are placed in order from left to right, with smaller numbers on the left and larger on the right. When looking at their numbers, is Mississippi to the left or right of the following?

    New York
    Hawaii
    West Virginia
    Ohio
    Texas
    Connecticut
    Maine
    South Dakota
4. Tell whether or not larger numbers represent the West Coast.
5. Tell how much larger the number for Montana is than the number for

    Michigan
    North Carolina
    New Hampshire
    Maryland
    Alabama
6. Put the 50 states in correct numerical order.

Assessment Criteria: The student will place the books in correct order and complete the worksheet.

■ ■ ■

Mathematics—Numbers

Media Skills Objective: Arrange materials using a specific system such as the *Dewey Decimal System of Classification.*

Level: 4-5

Learning Strategy: Game

Performance Objective: Given a series of Dewey numbers representing various sports, the students will arrange the numbers in the correct order.

Resources: Special worksheet and pencil.

Activity: After a brief explanation of the arrangement of the numbers, students will be given a worksheet with the following instructions: Connect the numbers. Using the chart, identify what subject the number represents. Find at least five titles for the numbers. What is the figure?

Figure 22

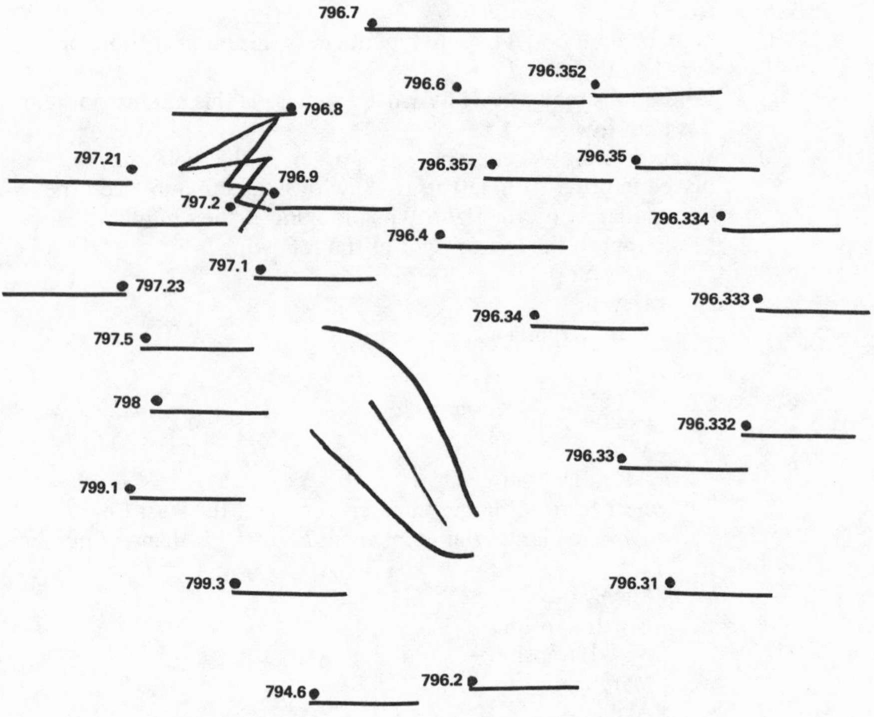

Mathematics—Numbers (cont'd)

Activity (cont'd)

Archery	799.3	_____
Baseball	796.357	_____
Basketball	796.32	_____
Bicycling	796.6	_____
Bowling	794.6	_____
Diving	797.2	_____
Fishing	799.1	_____
Football	796.332	_____
Handball	796.31	_____
Horseracing	798	_____
Golf	796.352	_____
Hockey	796.35	_____
Judo	796.8	_____
Pushball	796.33	_____
Racing	796.7	_____
Roller Skating	796.2	_____
Rugby	796.333	_____
Sailing	797.1	_____
Skiing	796.9	_____
Skin diving	797.23	_____
Sky diving	797.5	_____
Soccer	796.334	_____
Tennis	796.34	_____
Track	796.4	_____

Assessment Criteria: The student will complete the activity correctly.

■ ■ ■

Music—Musical Instruments

Media Skills Objective: Translate oral directions or written directions from a resource into a product or action.

Level: 1-4

Learning Strategy: Project

Performance Objective: Given written directions on how to make a musical instrument, the student will make a simple instrument.

Resources: *Childcraft*, make-it books, paper, cardboard, boxes, rubber bands, etc.

Activity: At a large table, set up simple directions for making various musical instruments. These instruments might include:

a. a whistle (paper)
b. a xylophone
c. a tom-tom

(List is continued on page 104.)

Music—Musical Instruments (cont'd)

Activity (cont'd)

- d. a tamborine
- e. rattles
- f. raspers
- g. nail chimes
- h. a kazoo
- i. gongs
- j. a cigar box guitar
- k. bell sticks
- l. a bottle xylophone

Sample: Rattle

1. Gather your materials:
   one long empty paper towel roll
   handful of dry beans
   one single piece of heavy paper for each end of the paper
   tube (5x5-inch)
   two heavy rubber bands
   paint and brush
2. Take the paper towel roll. If you wish you may paint a design on it.
3. Take one piece of paper.
4. Put the roll in the center of the paper.
5. Fold the paper down over the roll.
6. Put the rubber band around the end of the roll over the paper.
7. Put the beans in the roll.
8. Fix the other end of the roll as you did in steps 3—6.

Assessment Criteria: The student will follow the directions and make at least one musical instrument.

■   ■   ■

Reading and Language Arts—Animals

Media Skills Objective: Based on information from resources, compose a story which has a beginning, middle, and end.

Level: K-2

Learning Strategy: Practice

Performance Objective: Given specific information about snakes and the beginning of a story, the student will tell a complete story which has a beginning, middle, and an end.

Resources: An information book about snakes.

Activity: Using the resource book, the teacher will discuss with the students some of the characteristics of snakes and the composition of non-fiction stories based on factual information. Students should examine some of the pictures

Reading and Language Arts—Animals (cont'd)

Activity (cont'd)

in the book. Each student will be asked to make up a story about a snake after being given the beginning of a story. (Stories may also be written instead of recited.)

Example:

The small green snake lay coiled in the tall grass. The wind blew over the grass. He could feel it moving. Suddenly, he heard and felt heavy thumping noises . . . .

Assessment Criteria: The student will complete a story which has a beginning, middle, and an end.

■ ■ ■

Reading and Language Arts—Biography

Media Skills Objective: Use subject-oriented resources to find specific information.

Level: 6-8

Learning Strategy: Practice; game-puzzle

Performance Objective: Given eight last names of famous people and *Webster's Biographical Dictionary*, the student will find the complete names in order to finish the puzzle.

Resources: Puzzle, *Webster's Biographical Dictionary*, and a pencil.

Activity: Biographic Triplets
Directions:

The first names of these famous men are made up of triplets—groups of three letters—which may be taken from anywhere in the letter box illustrated below, reading from left to right. An example is G E O and R G E which spells George. Cross out the triplets in the box as you use them. Use *Webster's Biographical Dictionary* to identify the names. A few triplets will remain in the box. When properly arranged, they will form another name.

L	O	U	Q	U	I	A	R	D
U	E	L	R	O	B	G	E	O
N	C	Y	S	A	M	G	O	R
R	G	E	E	R	E	E	R	T
G	R	E	C	A	L	E	D	W
V	I	N	U	T	H	E	L	E

(Puzzle is continued on page 106.)

Reading and Language Arts—Biography (cont'd)

Activity (cont'd)

Names:

_____	Bruce — July 11, 1274
_____	Colt — July 19, 1814
_____	Eastman — July 12, 1854
_____	Gehrig — June 19, 1903
John _____	Adams — July 11, 1767
_____	Coolidge — July 4, 1872
_____	Dupont — June 24, 1771
_____	Grieg — June 15, 1843

Name left over: _____ Mendel

Assessment Criteria: The student will correctly complete the puzzle.

■ ■ ■

Reading and Language Arts—Fairy Tales (I)

Media Skills Objective: Compose a title for a story.

Level: K-2

Learning Strategy: Practice

Performance Objective: Given one fairy tale, the student will listen to the tale and give it a name.

Resources: A fairy tale which students have not heard before.

Activity: The students will listen to a fairy tale which they have never before heard. This story may be told to them with the book or put on tape. When the story is over, students will give the fairy tale a title which describes the story or some important aspect of it.

Example:

Rapunzel

Student title: _The Witch and the Princess with the Golden Hair_

Assessment Criteria: The student will produce a title.

■ ■ ■

Reading and Language Arts—Fairy Tales (II)

Media Skills Objectives: Identify and trace the development of a plot.

Illustrate a story or reading by making a series of pictures, clay figures, creative movements, etc.

Level: K-2

Learning Strategy: Role playing

Performance Objective: Given a set of familiar fairy tales written on a large wheel, the student will spin the wheel and act out the resulting story using a few props and other student actors as needed.

Resources: A large wheel listing fairy tales familiar to the students, props to match the stories.

Activity: Students will be prepared for the role playing by hearing several fairy tales. Those which might be included are:
1. Rapunzel
2. Three Billy Goats, Gruff
3. The Fisherman and His Wife
4. Snow White and the Seven Dwarfs
5. Snow White and Red Rose
6. Little Red Riding Hood
7. The Three Wishes
8. Rumpelstiltskin

On a wheel, put the name of each story. Students will spin the wheel and with others, act out the story.

For example:

If the story is "Little Red Riding Hood," the props might include a basket, red cloth for a hood, paper wolf ears, and a granny cap.

Assessment Criteria: The student will spin the wheel and use the props to act out the story. In acting out the story, the student will include the main incidents of the story.

■ ■ ■

Reading and Language Arts—Fantasy

Media Skills Objective: Identify specific information:
a. using visuals
b. listening to audio materials

Level: K-2

Learning Strategy: Discussion

Performance Objective: Given a flannel board set of stories about Winnie the Pooh and Christopher Robin, the student will identify various characters in the story who might be invited to a "Pooh" party.

Reading and Language Arts–Fantasy (cont'd)

Resources: Flannel board story figures of Winnie the Pooh.

Activity: Students will listen to a story of Winnie the Pooh and his friends. They will identify the characters in the story. The students will plan a party for Pooh and identify the characters who might come to it. The students will identify the food that various characters like to eat. After listening, students will prepare a menu for a "Pooh" party.

Assessment Criteria: The students will listen to the story and identify the characters and their diets.

■ ■ ■

Reading and Language Arts–Holidays; Valentine's Day, February 14

Media Skills Objectives: Identify and locate the card catalog.

Locate specific sources in the card catalog by author, title, or subject.

Locate specific information about an item on the catalog card.

Select resources using the card catalog and/or book catalog, given a specific subject, author, or title.

Locate a specific resource in the media center using the call number of the item given on a card catalog card.

Level: 4-6

Learning Strategy: Practice

Performance Objective: Given the name of a fellow student and an opportunity to observe that fellow student to determine interests, the student will:
1. identify a subject that interests the other student
2. use the card catalog to find materials on that subject
3. read the information on the catalog card which describes the information
4. select an item on that subject which seems suitable for the fellow student
5. locate the item, using the call number, to be sure the item is suitable.

Resources: Card catalog, media center materials, egg cartons, tempera paint, paper, pencil, and pipe cleaners.

Activity: Since Valentine's Day is a time for showing affection, the teacher can introduce an unusual kind of sharing. Students will be asked to exchange names and to keep it a secret. Each student will draw one name and observe the chosen person for a week. They will identify one subject in which the chosen student has shown some interest. The student will also determine the kind of material which the fellow student likes to use most (books, records, etc.). The subject of interest will be located in the card catalog. All items will be examined and one will be chosen. The students will note

Reading and Language Arts—Holidays;
Valentine's Day, February 14 (cont'd)

Activity (cont'd)

the call number and find the item to determine its suitability. Then the student will prepare a "buddy bouquet" of egg carton flowers for the person whose name was drawn. The egg cartons will be cut into a flower shape. The center of each flower will contain a yellow center listing either the author, title, call number, or a short blurb.

Illustration:

Figure 23

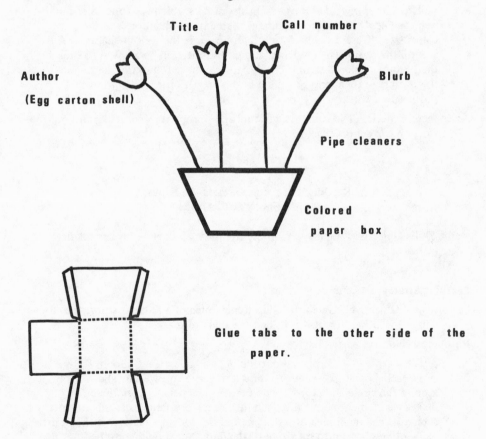

Assessment Criteria: The student will complete all parts of the activity and give the fellow student a "buddy bouquet."

■ ■ ■

Reading and Language Arts—Holidays;
St. Patrick's Day, March 17

Media Skills Objective: Identify and describe a written sequence of events.

Level: 2-5

Learning Strategy: Game

Performance Objective: Given segments of a story about St. Patrick's Day or related subjects, the student will put the segments in proper order.

Resources: Small shamrocks of different colors and a story.

Activity: Initiate a contest for small groups of students. Select a specific book such as *The Hungry Leprechan.* On shamrocks which are about 5x5-inch, write segments of the story. Put the segments on shamrocks of the same color. Use different colors for each group. Hide the various shamrocks around the room. The students, at a given time, will be allowed to look for their group's colored shamrocks. When they have found the shamrocks, they will read them and put them in the proper order. The group that finishes first wins.

Assessment Criteria: The students will find all appropriate shamrocks and put the story in correct order.

■ ■ ■

Reading and Language Arts—Holidays;
April Fool's Day, April 1

Media Skills Objective: Identify and describe the main idea in diverse media materials.

Level: 1-3

Learning Strategy: Game

Performance Objective: Given the alleged main idea of a familiar story, the student will tell whether or not it is in fact the main idea.

Resources: None in particular.

Activity: This game may be played outside or in a large area. Children form a large circle facing outward except for one who is the April Fool. The April Fool goes around the circle and stops at one person. The person from the circle makes a statement about the main idea of a story familiar to all students, such as, "The main idea of a story called *Bedtime for Frances* is that a little badger doesn't need to be afraid of the dark, but should go to bed on time." The April Fool tells whether or not the other student is "just foolin'." If the April Fool is correct, the two change places. If he is incorrect, both students run in opposite directions around the circle to see who can return to the spot first (April Fool to his right and the person in the circle to his right). The game continues.

Assessment Criteria: The student will correctly guess whether or not the alleged main idea is in fact the main idea.

Reading and Language Arts—Holidays;
National Children's Book Week or National Library Week (I)

Media Skills Objective: Identify and describe the theme or main issue of a narrative.

Level: 4

Learning Strategy: Reading, game

Performance Objective: Given an incentive to read ten books, the student will read the books and identify the main idea or theme of each.

Resources: Giant puzzle and a selection of fiction books.

Activity: To encourage reading in an entire class, sponsor a class contest. Take a large poster and cut it into ten times the number of students in the class. Students will each read ten books and identify the main idea of the book.

> Example: *Rabbit Hill* by Robert Lawson
> "Weaker creatures need to be protected so that they can survive."

They will report on their books when they have read them. When they have discussed the main issue or idea, they may select a puzzle piece to put in place.

Figure 24

(When the picture is cut apart, pieces will be numbered so they may be put in the correct place.)

1	2	3	4
5	6	7	8
9	10	11	12
13	14	15	16

The object is to complete the puzzle by a given date. When the puzzle is complete, it may be mounted.

Assessment Criteria: The students will read their books, giving the main idea of each.

■ ■ ■

Reading and Language Arts—Holidays;
National Children's Book Week or National Library Week (II)

Media Skills Objective: Predict consequences of actions and events in a narrative.

Level: 4-6

Learning Strategy: Reading, contract

Performance Objective: Given a book mutually read by the teacher and student, the student will prepare questions for the teacher on actions in the book and possible alternative consequences.

Resources: Book, paper, and pencil.

Activity: Make a contract with a student to read a specific book. Both will read the book. The student will agree to prepare some questions which might stump the teacher. The student will prepare at least five questions about various events in the book. The questions will deal with possible alternative consequences of the specific actions of characters. For each question, the student must also be prepared with an answer. Students may ask for predictions. (What if . . . . .)

Assessment Criteria: The student will meet the contract, i.e., he will submit five questions with possible answers.

■ ■ ■

Reading and Language Arts—Holidays;
Halloween, October 31

Media Skills Objectives: Identify and locate cassettes, cassette tape recorders, listening stations, and earphones.

Select an audio playing device for listening.

Select and match a cassette with a cassette tape recorder to play or record sounds.

Operate a listening station.

Operate a cassette tape recorder.

Select a listening station or earphones to individualize a listening experience.

Identify and describe an audio sequence of events.

Level: 1-3

Learning Strategy: Audiovisual Instruction

Performance Objective: Given a cassette taped sequence of "scary sounds," the student will locate a cassette tape recorder, use a listening station, and listen to the sounds in order to write a story which includes all of the sounds.

Reading and Language Arts—Holidays;
Halloween, October 31 (cont'd)

Resources: Sound effects recorded on a cassette tape (series might include wind, rain, thunder, running feet, knocking on the door, squeaking of an opening door, slam of a door, heavy breathing, thumping, creaking, steps up a stairs, etc.); a cassette tape recorder; a listening station; paper; and pencil.

Activity: The instructor will give the student the cassette tape with either written or oral instructions.
1.   Find a machine to use with this tape.
2.   Use a listening station.
3.   Play the tape.
4.   Listen to the sounds.
5.   Write a story when you have listened to the sounds.

(This can be done only if the student has previously been introduced to the equipment.)

Assessment Criteria: The student will follow all directions correctly and write a story that includes all of the sounds in their correct order.

■   ■   ■

Reading and Language Arts—Mythology

Media Skills Objectives: Identify and locate newspapers.

Select periodicals and newspapers for current information.

Use sections of a newspaper and its indexes to locate specific information for a definite purpose.

Level: 3-4

Learning Strategy: Individual project

Performance Objective: Given the story of Pandora and a newspaper, the student will use the newspaper to find items that might have flown out of Pandora's box.

Resources: Newspaper, paper, pencil, glue, story of Pandora.

Activity: The students will first read the story of Pandora. Their instructions after reading the story are to use the newspaper to find at least five headlines illustrating present-day "plagues, sorrows, and misfortunes." A short discussion may be necessary for students to consider what might be a plague, sorrow, or misfortune. On a dittoed chart with a picture of Pandora's box, students may paste their headlines as if the headlines were flying out of the box (see Figure 25 on page 114).

Reading and Language Arts—Mythology (cont'd)

Figure 25

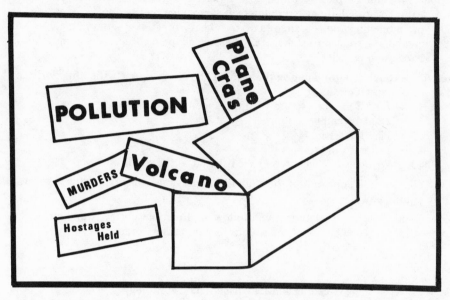

Assessment Criteria: The student will find at least five appropriate headlines and complete the activity.

■ ■ ■

Reading and Language Arts—Poetry

Media Skills Objectives: Prepare a handmade slide.

Use a chosen method involving lines, shapes, colors, and textures to express ideas, feelings, or experiences obtained from a resource.

Produce a media presentation that expresses a mood or feeling.

Prepare an audiovisual presentation.

Level: 2-6

Learning Strategy: Project

Performance Objective: Given directions on how to write particular kinds of poetry, materials to make handmade slides, and musical selections, the student will write a poem, prepare handmade slides, and match the music to the slides.

Resources: Directions for writing Haiku, Senryu, Cinquain, Tanka, and Diamente poetry; clear plastic acetate; laminating film; A-V pencils; colored tissue paper; tacking iron; dry mount press; records; record players; and slide mounts.

Reading and Language Arts—Poetry (cont'd)

Activity: This project involves several parts. The student will write a Haiku, Senryu, Cinquain, Tanka, or Diamente poem. As an introduction, the teacher will take some poems from various Japanese poetry books, make hand-made nature slides to accompany the poems, and play suitable music as the slides are projected and the poetry read.

After the introduction, students will receive directions for writing their poems.

Haiku—subject must deal with nature; contains 17 syllables in 3 lines
Line 1, five syllables
Line 2, seven syllables
Line 3, five syllables
(The lines do not rhyme; they answer where, what, and when.)

Senryu—subject is not limited to nature; contains 17 syllables in three lines
Line 1, five syllables
Line 2, seven syllables
Line 3, five syllables

Cinquain—five lines
Line 1, one word subject, title
Line 2, two descriptive words
Line 3, three action words
Line 4, four feeling words
Line 5, one word, synonym for the title

Tanka—subject is about nature or the seasons; contains 31 syllables in five lines
Line 1, five syllables; one subject
Line 2, seven syllables; one subject
Line 3, five syllables; second subject
Line 4, seven syllables; second subject
Line 5, seven syllables; refrain

Diamente—seven lines in a diamond shape
Line 1, one word title or subject
Line 2, two adjectives
Line 3, three participles (-ing, -ed)
Line 4, four nouns related to subject (last two related to line 7)
Line 5, three participles (related to line 7)
Line 6, two adjectives (related to line 7)
Line 7, one noun (opposite line 1)

When the students have written their poems, they are ready to make their slides. This involves laying out the slides on a sheet of paper first (see Figure 26 on page 116).

Reading and Language Arts—Poetry (cont'd)

Activity (cont'd)

Figure 26

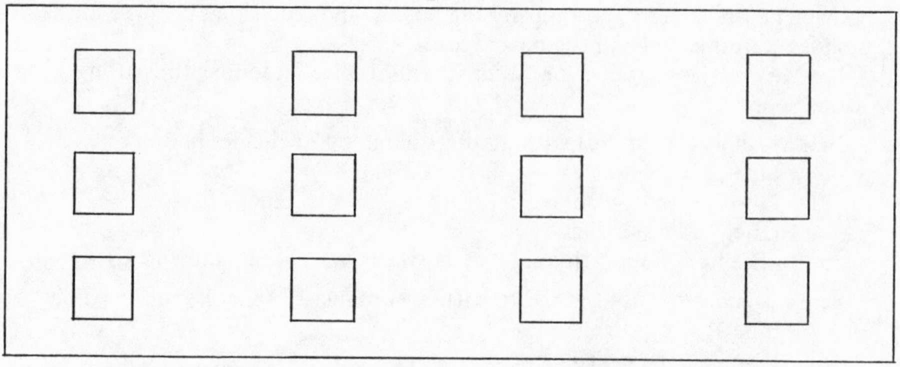

After students have determined what should be included in their slides (e.g., drawings, tiny leaves and tissue paper, feathers, etc.), the actual slides are ready to be made. The clear acetate will be placed over the paper and materials will be placed on the acetate. Next, the acetate will be covered with laminated film, and a tacking iron or dry mount press is used to mount the slides, which can then be cut out and placed into slide mounts.

The students will then select records or music to accompany the poems and slides. The slides will be placed in sequence, music played, and the poem read.

Assessment Criteria: The student will complete the project as described.

■   ■   ■

Science—Animals (I)

Media Skills Objective: Identify and describe a pictorial sequence of events.

Level: 3-6

Learning Strategy: Learning center

Performance Objective: Given four different sets of animal track sequences, the student will tell what the animal did to make that sequence of tracks.

Resources: One book of animal tracks, such as *A Field Guide to Animal Tracks* by Olaus Murie, one learning center area which includes four plaster casts of animal tracks (tracks may also be drawn on poster paper), paper, and pencil.

Activity: A learning center area will be set up consisting of four activities. The teacher will prepare four plaster of Paris molds. In each mold, footprints will be arranged to show a possible sequence of events. Students will go to each, view the mold, determine the animals that made the tracks (using

Science—Animals (I) (cont'd)

Activity (cont'd)

the track book), and then describe from the molded track sequence what they think happened to the animals.

Suggested sequences:
1. Jack rabbit sitting; running; then tracks ending abruptly (captured by a hawk).
2. Field mouse walking, sitting by corn kernels, running in opposite direction.
3. Mole tracks hurrying toward hole, dog tracks following.
4. Bird tracks by a puddle, cat tracks showing running and pouncing.

At each activity, the student should complete this paper:

Sequence
1. Animal or animals _____
2. Description of event _____
   _____

When the student finishes each sequence, an answer card will be made available for student comparison and checking.

If the teacher is an outdoors fan, real tracks may be copied. Directions for preserving tracks may be found in *A Field Guide to Animal Tracks* on pages 5-8.

Assessment Criteria: The student will complete all four sequences with at least 50 percent accuracy.

■　■　■

Science—Animals (II)

Media Skills Objective: Use an encyclopedia to locate specific information.

Level: 4

Learning Strategy: Game; practice

Performance Objective: Given the appropriate volume of the *Merit Students Encyclopedia*, the student will locate specific information about cats in order to complete a crossword puzzle (Figure 27, page 118).

Resources: *Merit Students Encyclopedia*; pencil; a crossword puzzle.

Activity: Use the *Merit Students Encyclopedia* to complete the crossword puzzle.

Science—Animals (II) (cont'd)

Figure 27

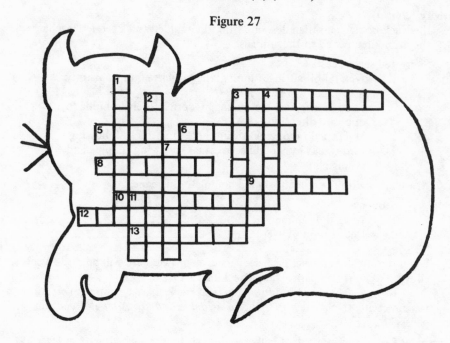

Across

3—meat-eating animal
5—tailless cat
6—origin of this breed remains a
    mystery
8—term applied to all gray cats
9—tortoise-shell colored cat
10—breed which likes water
12—fish which cats like to eat
13—breed originating in Thailand

Down

1—long-haired cat developed by
    by the British
2—only curly-haired breed of cat
3—pale cream-colored coat of a cat
4—_____ Blue, a breed of cat
7—breed resembles a pekingese dog
9—lions belong to the _____
    family
11—Egyptian goddess with head of cat

Assessment Criteria: The student will complete the crossword puzzle with no errors. Puzzle answers are shown in Figure 28.

Figure 28

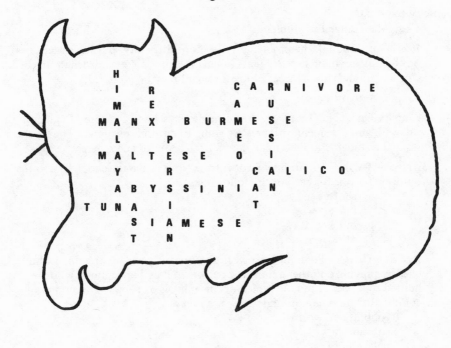

• • •

Science—Ecology

Media Skills Objectives: Define a problem for research.

Plan a method of solving a problem using reference source.

Level: 5-8

Learning Strategy: Learning center

Performance Objective: Given a set of problems, the student will define them and present a plan for solving them using specific reference tools.

Resources: An artificial tree on which to hang problem cards, set of 20 problem cards, paper, and pencil.

Activity: A large artificial tree will be set up with large letters saying "ECOLOGY" or "ENVIRONMENT." Hanging from the branches will be 20 or more ecology problems about which students need to find more information. These problems deal with a need for specific information. Students will be given instructions to select at least five problems one at a time. They will:

1. define the problem
2. determine what it is that might help them solve that problem
3. give a written description of how they might go about solving that problem using specific reference tools or skills

Science—Ecology (cont'd)

Activity (cont'd)

    4.   solve the problem

It is helpful to rank the problems by levels of difficulty, putting easier ones on the bottom branches. Students rehang their problem cards when finished. (Instead of an artificial tree, a bulletin board may be prepared.)

Sample Activity Cards:

Activity One: There is a large tree outside the school. Because of cracks in the sidewalk and pavement, officials are going to cut the tree down. The teachers want the students to determine how far the roots go and where.

Activity Two: Find out how far it is from your home to school. Try to figure out how far it is for each of the following:

    1.   shortest way
    2.   longest way
    3.   quickest way
    4.   safest way

Activity Three: "Predator" is a word that means a person or animal who lives by preying on other animals or persons. "Prey" are animals who are hunted by others. Find out which of the animals or people common in the community are predators and which are prey:

    robbins and worms
    cats and rats
    gulls and fish
    lizards and mosquitos
    borrowers and loan companies
    landlords and tenants

Find out how these relationships can be changed. How will the balance of the environment be affected if any of the predators or prey are removed? What will happen if the prey becomes the predator?

Activity Four: What is the difference between conservation and preservation? Find five examples in the environment around you that show conservation and five examples that show preservation.

Activity Five: What are national parks? Determine the location of the national parks in the United States. Identify the origin of the national park system and five of the parks in the system. Explain the maintenance of the national parks.

Activity Six: Investigate the following men's lives:

    1.   John Audubon
    2.   Daniel Beard
    3.   Hugh Bennett
    4.   Bernard Fernow
    5.   George Grinell
    6.   William Hornsday
    7.   George Marsh
    8.   Sterling Morton

(List is continued on page 121.)

Science—Ecology (cont'd)

Activity (cont'd)

9. John Muir
10. Gifford Pinchot
11. John Powell
12. Ernest Seton
13. Charles Van Hise

Show the contributions they have made to the conservation effort.

Activity Seven: Using nonprint materials, show a large group of students some of the endangered species.

Activity Eight: Find a copy of the Clean Air Act (1963) or information on the Act. Find a way to show what the Act attempts to accomplish.

Activity Nine: Determine the most common geometric shape in your environment:

triangle	parallelogram
circle	rectangle
square	trapezoid

Activity Ten: Determine the amount of traffic that passes your school. Count the number of cars and trucks that pass your school for 20 minutes for each of five days. Make a graphic representation of your information.

Activity Eleven: Many people cannot read, but need to know about pollution and conservation. Find a way to demonstrate the meaning to some of these words:

pollution	watershed
conservation	oxygen
preservation	transpiration
interdependence	chlorination
adaptation	fluoridation
silt	respiration
filtration	distillation
irrigation	erosion
industry	detergents
aeration	reservoirs
desalinization	

Activity Twelve: Compare rainmakers of old with present-day cloud seeders.

Activity Thirteen: Show the wildlife prevalent in your area and its natural habitat by preparing a poster or chart.

Activity Fourteen: Provide a visual representation of various classifications of animals such as:

1. Animals with Feathers
2. Game Animals
3. Animals Which Help Man
4. Animals Which Provide Us with Food
5. etc.

Science—Ecology (cont'd)

Activity (cont'd)

Activity Fifteen: Investigate the causes of the Dust Bowl and the reasons for strip mining.

Activity Sixteen: Pretend that you are a member of a citizens' group which is fighting to save a local stream polluted daily by sewage. You have joined a larger group that is trying to encourage water pollution legislation. Show how you would gather evidence to present to others.

Activity Seventeen: Illustrate the farming methods of early cultures. (Include the Egyptians, Romans, Mayans, Incas, etc.)

Activity Eighteen: Examine the school grounds. Locate areas of soil erosion and determine methods of preventing it.

Activity Nineteen: Without leaving your school, study a river in or near your community. Trace the course of the river from its source. Give the names of other communities by which the river flows.

Activity Twenty: Identify the names of all lakes and rivers in your area. Prepare a guide for others to show what is available at that location and note the condition of the water. Show whether or not it is polluted, fit for drinking, swimming, or boating.

Assessment Criteria: The student will correctly define the five problems and give a possible method of solving each.

Example for Activity One:
1. Show the location of the roots
2. Map of the roots
3. Observe signs of the root system and prepare a map to scale of that system.

■ ■ ■

Science—Pets

Media Skills Objectives: Use an encyclopedia to locate specified information.

Skim materials to find the answer to a given question.

Compare ideas found in resources for similarity, identity, difference, and contradiction.

Operate an opaque projector.

Compare facts, ideas, and visual images from more than one source.

Level: 6

Learning Strategy: Group project

Performance Objectives: Given a list of pets and a set of encyclopedias, the student will find information on five of the pets listed.

Given an encyclopedia article for each of the five chosen pets, the student will skim each article to identify the diet of each.

Science—Pets (cont'd)

Performance Objectives (cont'd)

Given one chosen pet and its diet, the student will examine at least two sample pet foods, comparing them for contents, weight, nutrients, and price.

Given sample pet food labels, the student will use an opaque projector to enlarge the labels for discussion with other students.

Given information on the chosen pet's diet from the encyclopedia and two sample foods, the student will compare the two to see which of the two is nutritionally superior.

Resources: Sets of encyclopedias, worksheets listing pets, pet food labels, opaque projector, and pencil.

Activity: This project is divided into five parts. The teacher introduces the project by discussing the importance of the food we eat as well as that which animals eat.

Parts I and II: The students will be given a list of pets. They will locate five animals in the encyclopedia and specify their diets.

Pet	Food	Pet	Food
Dog		Horse	
Cat		Duck	
Guppy		Rabbit	
Goldfish		Chicken	
Gerbil		Snake	
Mouse		Guinea pig	

Part III: The students will select one pet and collect appropriate pet food labels. They will then divide into groups according to the pets chosen. After they discuss in their groups the recommended food for their chosen pets, they will examine at least two appropriate labels for content, nutritive value, weight, and price.

Parts IV and V: Groups will report their findings to all other groups using the opaque projector. They will discuss their findings and compare:

a. two labels for pet food chosen for
    content _____
    weight _____
    nutritive value _____
    price _____

b. two sample labels with ideal contents (determined by encyclopedia research) to select the best commercial food.

Diet (Encyclopedia)	Label One	Label Two

Assessment Criteria: The student will participate in each part of the project and will correctly complete each part selecting the best commercial pet food for his chosen pet.

■   ■   ■

Science—Plants

Media Skills Objective: Use subject-oriented resources to find specific information.

Use more than one source to gather information.

Prepare a report using one chosen medium.

Level: 6-8

Learning Strategy: Individual project

Performance Objective: Given the name of a flower and various resources, the student will prepare an illustrated project on "The Secret or Private Life of (flower chosen)."

Resources: Reference tools, professional tools such as *The Secret Life of Plants* by Peter Tompkins and Christopher Bird, paper, and pencil.

Activity: After an opening discussion on plants, students will do research on the growth of the flower chosen, its environment and growth requirements. Students will then write and illustrate a project called the "Secret or Private Life of a Rose," etc., depending on their choice. Gardening books will be necessary for reference. Before students prepare their project, their teacher or media specialist may want to discuss how students might approach their work (point of view, personification, etc.).

Assessment Criteria: The student will use more than one subject-oriented resource to complete a report on "The Secret or Private Life of a Rose," etc.

■ ■ ■

Science—Weather (I)

Media Skills Objectives: Identify and locate copying machines.

Operate a copy machine.

Prepare a machine-made transparency.

Level: 6-8

Learning Strategy: Project

Performance Objective: Given five consecutive days of weather reports from a newspaper, the student will prepare machine-made transparencies of each day's report to show weather changes.

Resources: Copy machine, appropriate transparency paper, transparency mounts, scissors, masking tape, newspaper weather reports, and hinges.

Activity: In order for students to understand weather symbols and the movement of high and low pressure systems, have them collect the weather maps and reports from the newspaper for five consecutive days. When students have collected their maps, they will follow the machine directions and make five transparencies. When the transparencies have been completed, they will be

Science—Weather (I) (cont'd)

Activity (cont'd)

mounted as a single transparency with four overlays. The overlays will indicate the weather changes and the movement of high and low pressure systems.

Example:

Figure 29

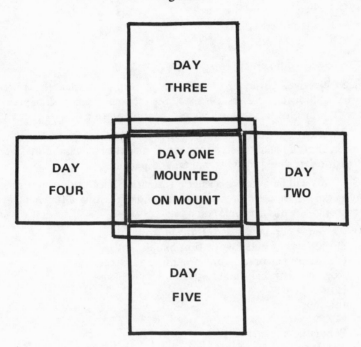

Assessment Criteria: The student will complete the transparency with overlays.

■ ■ ■

Science—Weather (II)

Media Skills Objectives: Identify and locate cassettes.

Identify and locate cassette tape recorders.

Select and match a cassette with a cassette tape recorder to play or record sounds.

Identify and locate slides.

Identify and locate slide previewers.

Identify and locate slide projectors.

Science—Weather (II) (cont'd)

Media Skills Objectives (cont'd)

Select and match slides with a slide projector to show a series of visuals.

Operate a cassette tape recorder.

Operate a slide previewer.

Record information on a cassette tape recorder.

Prepare a slide.

Prepare a slide presentation.

Level: 6-8

Learning Strategy: Audiovisual project

Performance Objective: Given information on the winter solstice, the student will identify and locate cassettes, cassette tape recorders, slides, slide previewer, and slide projector to prepare a slide/tape presentation.

Resources: Information sources about the winter solstice, cassette, cassette tape recorder, film to make slides, slides, visual maker or camera to make slides, slide previewer, slide projector, paper, and pencil.

Activity: Students will be asked to gather information about the winter solstice. Many peoples have celebrated this with holiday feasting. Students will find the customs of various people, such as:

> Ancient Egyptians' use of lotus blossoms
> Druids' use of yule logs or fires in oak groves
> Christians' celebration of Christmas and Epiphany
> Romans' Saturnalia and mistletoe
> Hopi Indians
> Eskimos
> Chinese New Year
> Polynesians
> Northern Scandinavians
> Hindus Pongol of the Cows

When students have gathered information, they can prepare a script for slides.

Figure 30

Slides	Narrative

The type of slide to be shown should be identified beside the narrative. The students then will take their pictures. They will follow the schedule listed:

Science—Weather (II) (cont'd)

Activity (cont'd)

1. Correct the script.
2. Identify the slides.
3. Take the slides necessary. (Follow the instructions for equipment used, such as the Visualmaker.)
4. Have slides developed.
5. Arrange the slides in the proper sequence.
6. Record the tape. (Bell sounds may be put on the recording to indicate slide changes.)
7. Show the presentation.

Assessment Criteria: The student will complete the tape and slides and show the finished presentation.

■ ■ ■

Social Studies—Black Americans

Media Skills Objectives: Identify and locate specific periodicals.

Support research on a given question using specified resource materials.

Level: 6-8

Learning Strategy: Reading; group project

Performance Objectives: Given the dates 1965-1975 and the name of a periodical (*Newsweek*), the student will locate all available issues.

Given seven categories such as Sports, Politics, Medicine, Invention, Arts and Entertainment, Fashion, and Finance, the student will examine magazine issues and list prominent people by year in each listed category, comparing yearly listings to see if there has been a quantitative change in Black involvement.

Resources: Worksheet with categories listed, back issues of *Newsweek* (1965-1975), and pencil.

Activity: Students will be asked to determine if there has been an increase in Black involvement in listed categories since the middle '60s. Before they answer, they must be able to substantiate their opinion. They will be asked to do this by using *Newsweek* magazine from 1965 to 1975. Students are to use the selected categories and list findings by years.

	1965	1966	1967	1968	1969	1970	1971	etc.
Politics								
Sports								
Medicine								
Invention								
Arts and Entertainment								
Fashion								
Finance								

Social Studies—Black Americans (cont'd)

Activity (cont'd)

They will use at least two issues from each year.

When students have completed their studies, their information will be pooled into one large chart. They will again be asked if they can see a change in the ten-year period. Students are then grouped to discuss the question and possible reasons for the answer.

Assessment Criteria: Students will find appropriate periodicals, use at least two issues from each year, complete the required data gathering, and pool their data with that of the whole class to answer the question.

■ ■ ■

Social Studies—Communication (I)

Media Skill Objectives: Select an encyclopedia to find information on a given subject.

Identify and locate encyclopedias.

Identify and locate guide words in a print item.

Find specific information in materials using guide words.

Skim materials to find an answer to a question.

Select and distinguish among volumes of an encyclopedia which is arranged alphabetically to find information on a given topic.

Use an encyclopedia to solve a problem.

Level: 3-5

Learning Strategy: Discussion; project

Performance Objective: Given the problem of decoding a message in Morse Code, the student will select an encyclopedia, select the correct volume of the set, use guide words, and skim to find the code and decode the message.

Resources: Set of encyclopedias, Morse Code message, and pencil.

Activity: The teacher will first introduce the lesson with a discussion of codes and ciphers as a means of communication. The discussion will lead to an identification of the need for codes. Students will then be given the copy of the first message sent by telegraph.

Decode this message. It is the first telegraph message sent by the inventor of the telegraph, Samuel Morse.

.─ ── .... .─ ─ .... .─ ─ ....

──. ─── ─.. .─ ─ .─. ─── ..─ ──. .... ─

The students will be given the following instructions:

You are to find one encyclopedia in the media center in which Morse's Code may be found. When this encyclopedia is located,

Social Studies—Communication (I) (cont'd)

Activity (cont'd)

give the title of the encyclopedia, the volume number, the page, and guide words (if any), and then use the code to decode the message. After finishing, you may prepare a message to send.

Assessment Criteria: The student will identify the encyclopedia, volume, page, guide words, and give the decoded message, "What hath God wrought."

■ ■ ■

Social Studies—Communication (II)

Media Skills Objective: Find specific information in materials using:
a. guide words
b. headings and subheadings
c. key words and phrases

Level: 4-6

Learning Strategy: Group project

Performance Objective: Given an encyclopedia article on communication, the student will find information on the subject using the guide words, headings and subheadings, and key words and phrases.

Resources: Article on communication from an encyclopedia such as *The World Book Encyclopedia*, large diagram on the bulletin board, scissors, old magazines, and tacks.

Activity: The teacher will prepare a large bulletin board space with one word in the center—"COMMUNICATION." Around the word, lines branch out, ending with spaces for subheadings and pictures of those subheadings. The subheadings in turn are provided with branching lines for key words, phrases, and appropriate pictures.

Figure 31

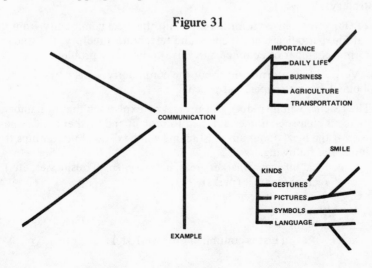

Social Studies—Communication (II) (cont'd)

Activity (cont'd)

The teacher will discuss the article and its headings with the students, showing them where the headings branch from the main topic. Students will select one section of the article and find at least two ideas or words that relate to the heading. Students will fill in the spaces with the appropriate words and phrases for each heading or subheading. They will also cut pictures to represent the words. When the board is completed, the teacher and students may begin a discussion of the word and pictures.

Assessment Criteria: Students will locate the headings and subheadings and find at least two key words under each subheading.

■ ■ ■

Social Studies—Community

Media Skills Objectives: Identify and locate the vertical file.

Select the vertical file as a source of pamphlet information.

Identify and locate:
a.   periodicals
b.   newspapers
c.   the telephone directory

Select periodicals and newspapers for current information.

Select a telephone directory to find correct numbers to be dialed.

Use a telephone directory.

Use sections of a newspaper and its indexes to locate specific information for a defined purpose.

Level: 3-7

Learning Strategy: Project

Performance Objective: Given information about the local community from the vertical file, periodicals, newspapers, and telephone directory, the students will form a chamber of commerce to solve community problems.

Resources: Vertical file information about the community, local newspapers, telephone directory, paper, and pencil.

Activity: The teacher will introduce this project by explaining that a chamber of commerce is an association established to protect and further the business interests of the local community. Students will be divided into groups to determine the following:
1.   local business (market areas, industry, small businesses, etc.)
2.   recreation areas (parks)
3.   government agencies
4.   churches
5.   schools

(List is continued on page 131.)

Social Studies—Community (cont'd)

Activity (cont'd)

6. type of geographical area and homes
7. utilities
8. transportation

The students will use the vertical file information, newspapers, and yellow pages of the telephone directory to gather their information. The information will be gathered by a group leader and shared with all other groups when completed. The students then will be asked to identify businesses that might belong to a chamber of commerce in their community. Students will next identify the community interests. A problem may be given to the students and each can represent a business or group and deal with that community problem.

Assessment Criteria: Students will include 50 percent of the members of a chamber of commerce (if it exists) or 50 percent of potential members if one did exist, using the vertical file, periodicals, newspapers, and the telephone directory.

■ ■ ■

Social Studies—Early Man

Media Skills Objectives: Identify and describe:

a. a pictorial sequence of events
b. an audio sequence of events

Level: 2-4

Learning Strategy: Audiovisual instruction

Performance Objective: Given a series of pictures on prehistoric man and an audio story that follows the pictures, the student will listen to the story, look at the pictures, and when the pictures are disarranged, will put them back in proper order.

Resources: One taped story about a day in the life of early man, pictures to accompany the audio narrative, and a tape recorder.

Activity: The student will listen to the taped story following the pictures. When the student has finished listening, the pictures will be shuffled. The student will then put the pictures back in order and orally describe the sequence. This oral sequence may be taped by the student or heard directly by the instructor.

Assessment Criteria: The student will put the pictures in correct sequence after listening to the audio sequence.

■ ■ ■

Social Studies—Economics

Media Skills Objective: Skim materials to find a word, name, date, phrase, sentence, idea, or answer to a question.

Level: 4

Learning Strategy: Reading; discussion

Performance Objective: Given a short factual narrative on a country and its products, the student will skim the material in two minutes to determine the name of the country and its main products and tell others the findings.

Resources: Short set of readings on countries and their products (exports).

Activity: The teacher will inform the students that they are going to hold a short international fair to do some trading. Each student will be given a different duplicated book page or pamphlet which describes a country and its products. The students will be given two minutes to skim their information and name their particular country and its main products. (Before beginning the next step, the teacher should make sure that all students have their information.)

When this has been completed, students will walk around and, as in a market place, shout out or sell their product. An opportunity may be given to them to compose a rhyme about their product.

When students have circulated among themselves for a short time, they will be called back together. Students will identify the countries and products of others and a composite listing will be made.

Assessment Criteria: Students will identify the correct country and product within two minutes. (The article cannot be entirely read in two minutes.)

■ ■ ■

Social Studies—Egypt, Ancient (I)

Media Skills Objectives: Select non-fiction materials for an account of factual or "real" information and occurrences.

Identify a fact, truth, reality, or possibility in a source.

Skim to find material relevant to a topic.

Level: 4-7

Learning Strategy: Small group project

Performance Objective: Given a collection of books and other materials about Egypt, the student will select the non-fiction materials and skim to find facts about Egyptian cosmetics.

Resources: Collection of books and materials about ancient Egypt, paper, cardboard, bottles, and pencil.

Social Studies—Egypt, Ancient (I) (cont'd)

Activity: The teacher will explain to students that they are to draw plans for an ancient Egyptian grooming center. Students will need to be sure they understand for what they are searching (cosmetics, beauty aids, grooming, hairdressing, etc.). Students will identify what cosmetics the Egyptians used and draw plans for a center of grooming. Empty bottles may be labeled with the names of cosmetics. Chairs and mirrors may be placed in the plans. Cardboard or stiff paper combs and other identified items used in grooming may be diagrammed.

Assessment Criteria: The student will select at least two non-fiction books and skim to identify at least five of the following items:
    bath tub
    kohl stick (for eyes)
    green malachite eye shadow
    henna for nails, palms of hands, and feet
    lip paint
    skin lotion
    ivory eye liner stick
    bronze mirror
    hair curlers (hair was curled or plaited)
    compounds derived from thyme, origanum, balanos, myrrh,
        frankincense, spikenard, sesame oil, almond oil, and olive oil
    perfumed bath oil

The student will draw a sample plan for the arrangement of beauty aids.

■ ■ ■

Social Studies—Egypt, Ancient (II)

Media Skills Objectives: Identify and locate an appendix in a print item.

Use an appendix to locate material and information.

Level: 5-7

Learning Strategy: Reading; practice

Performance Objective: Given a book on ancient Egypt with an appendix and a worksheet listing problems related to ancient Egypt, the student will find the appendix and use it to complete the worksheet.

Resources: Book with appendix (*Land of the Pharaohs* by Leonard Cottrell), worksheet, and pencil.

Activity: The teacher will introduce the concept of an appendix and time line. The student will be instructed to complete the worksheet. The worksheet is to be used with the book *Land of the Pharaohs*, by Leonard Cottrell.

Worksheet
This exercise deals with events that occurred in ancient Egypt between the years 4000 B.C. and 500 A.D. It also asks questions comparing events that occurred in other parts of the world. It would be helpful to have a time

Social Studies—Egypt, Ancient (II) (cont'd)

Activity (cont'd)

line. Does this book have a section which might give helpful information to answer these questions? _____

If so, what is this section called? _____

In what section of the book is it located? _____

What is this section usually called? _____

Use this section of the book to answer the following questions:

1. What ruler of Egypt died about 1350 B.C. after the peak of ancient civilization? _____
2. When did the Exodus of Jews from Egypt occur? _____
3. Did Cleopatra live during the time when Egypt was ruled by Nubians? _____
4. What conqueror of Egypt founded the capital at Alexandria? When? _____
5. From the chart, tell what was happening in the Near East, Africa, and Asia when Menes united the Nile Valley people.
    _____
6. What was happening in Egypt around the time of the Golden age of the Hittite Civilization (1400 B.C.)? _____
    _____
    _____
7. The warrior kings of Egypt drove the foreigners from Egypt before/ after the Fall of Troy in Europe? _____

Assessment Criteria: The student will find the appendix and answer the questions correctly.

Answers:

Yes

Chronological Chart of Ancient Egypt and World Events

Back of the book

Appendix

1. Tutankhamen
2. About 1200 B.C.
3. No
4. Alexander the Great, 332 B.C.
5. City state civilizations develop from farming settlements in Tigris-Euphrates—Near East
    First farmers in the Indus Valley—Asia
6. The Valley of Kings replaced the pyramids.
    The Temple of Amen Re was built at Karnak.
7. Before

■   ■   ■

Social Studies—Family Life

Media Skills Objectives: Identify and describe a pictorial sequence of events.

Prepare a handmade filmstrip.

Level: K-3

Learning Strategy: Individual project

Performance Objective: Given a family event and materials to prepare a filmstrip, the student will identify and pictorially describe the family event on a hand-made filmstrip.

Resources: U-film (blank 35mm film), colored pencils, stencil for drawing pictures.

Activity: Students will first be asked to think about their families and identify family members. They will then be asked to describe an incident which occurred in their family. When they have described an incident, they may take a sheet of paper on which a filmstrip stencil has been reproduced. They next draw the family event on the paper in proper sequence. When students have finished their drawings, they may draw their pictures on the u-film with audiovisual pencils (Figure 32). Students may show their filmstrips and describe the incident.

Figure 32

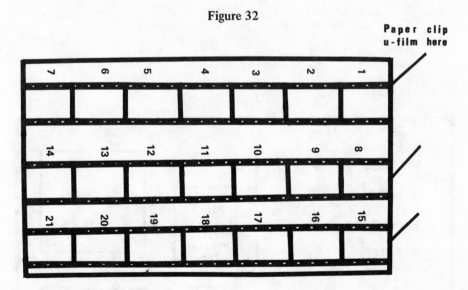

Assessment Criteria: Students will describe an incident and complete a filmstrip depicting the incident.

■ ■ ■

Social Studies—Food

Media Skills Objective: Draw or infer conclusions on a given topic from more than one source.

Level: 6

Learning Strategy: Learning center

Performance Objective: Given a newspaper, community or city map, United States map, telephone directory, almanac, and encyclopedia, the student will draw conclusions about the places from which our food originates.

Resources: Learning center, copies of activities, pencils, daily newspaper with food advertisements, community or city map, United States map, telephone directory, almanac, encyclopedia, and sample plastic foods or pictures of foods.

Activity: Prepare a large center as indicated in Figure 33. Components of the center include:
1. a brown paper bag with plastic food or pictures of food in it
2. a map of the immediate community
3. a simple map of the United States
4. general student directions:
   a. Examine all of the activities.
   b. Start with the first one of the activities.
   c. Complete the activity. (Sometimes you will find several parts.)
   d. Have your completed work evaluated by your media specialist or teacher.

Figure 33

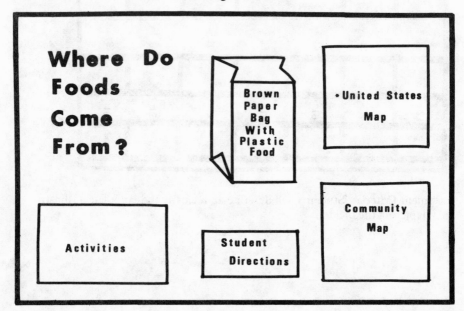

Social Studies—Food (cont'd)

Activity (cont'd)

Activity One:
1. Examine the food in the brown paper bag.
2. Identify all of the items.
3. Find a copy of your local newspaper.
4. Find the food advertisements. (Use the index if necessary.)
5. Find the prices for the food items in the brown paper bag.
6. Find the food advertisements for four different stores and find prices for foods at those stores.
7. Compare the food prices. At what stores would you probably want to buy these foods? Why?

Activity Two:
1. Find a map of your city and your local neighborhood.
2. Examine your newspaper and identify all of the grocery stores that advertise in that newspaper.
3. Find a copy of the telephone directory.
4. Locate the names of these stores in your telephone directory.
5. Identify the telephone number and address.
6. Using your local map or city map, find the five grocery stores closest to your home.
7. From information found in Activity One, tell which store close to your home has the best buys on the food samples in the brown bag.

Activity Three:
1. Find an almanac.
2. Identify the food in the packet and divide it into categories such as:
   Vegetables
   Fruit
   Cereal (Wheat, Rye, Corn, etc.)
   Eggs
   Meat (Bacon, Pork, etc.)
3. Using the index in the almanac, find the chart or graph that will tell you which state in the United States produces the most of each type of food.
4. List the information you have found.
5. What states produce small quantities of each type of food?
6. Choose two items and tell from which states these may have come.

Activity Four:
1. From the foods in the brown paper bag, identify types of food people eat for breakfast.
2. Use the encyclopedia to discover where these foods grow best. Identify the type of soil the plants need in order to grow. Identify the areas of the United States where this type of soil must be located, since they produce the foods identified.

Social Studies—Food (cont'd)

Activity (cont'd)

3. Do the same activities for three foods which are more likely to be eaten at dinner than at breakfast time.

Answer cards will be prepared so that students may check their own work.

Assessment Criteria: The student will complete the activities with at least 60 percent accuracy.

■ ■ ■

Social Studies—Greece, Ancient (I)

Media Skills Objectives: Distinguish between fact and fiction.

Identify:
a. fantasy, unreality, impossibility, and incongruity in a resource
b. a fact, truth, reality, or possibility in a resource

Level: 4-6

Learning Strategy: Discussion, practice

Performance Objectives: Given five books on Greek mythology, five factual books on ancient Greece, and five fiction books on ancient Greece, the student will identify those books which are factual and those which are fiction.

Given excerpts from each of the fifteen books, the student will identify whether or not each excerpt is fact or fiction.

Resources: List of fifteen books, paper, and pencil.

Activity: In several lessons, the students will read and discuss mythology as well as real events in ancient Athens. They will view filmstrips such as *Life in Ancient Athens* by McGraw-Hill and listen to stories such as "Midas and the Golden Touch." After these lessons, fifteen books will be placed on a table including the following titles:

938	Mills, D. *The Book of the Ancient Greeks*
Fic	Cone, M. *Green, Green Sea*
292	Hamilton, E. *Mythology*
938	Rockwell, A. *Temple on a Hill*
Fic	Fenton, E. *Island for a Pelican*
292	Hawthorne, N. *The Golden Touch*
292	Sellew, C. *Adventures with the Gods*
938	Coolidge, O. *The Golden Days of Greece*
292	Bulfinch, T. *A Book of Myths*
Fic	Wuorio, E. *Kali and the Golden Mirror*
292	Coolidge, O. *Greek Myths*
709.38	Price, C. *Made in Ancient Greece*
Fic	Corbett, S. *Cave above Delphi*
709.34	Glubok, S. *The Art of Ancient Greece.*

Social Studies—Greece, Ancient (I) (cont'd)

Activity (cont'd)

The student will be asked to:

1. determine which books are fact and which are fiction (Students may look at blurbs, examine tables of contents, or skim.)

2. read pages marked in each book to identify fantasy and facts in the excerpt marked.

Assessment Criteria: The student will complete the activity with at least 60 percent accuracy.

■ ■ ■

Social Studies—Greece, Ancient (II)

Media Skills Objectives: Select a visual projection device for examining pictures.

Locate specific information using visuals.

Illustrate a story or reading by making a series of pictures, clay figures, creative movements, etc.

Level: 6-8

Learning Strategy: Project

Performance Objective: Given a factual account of everyday life in ancient Athens, the student will find pictures, filmstrips, and slides about the account, pick out information from the pictures, and prepare a cameo of the reading.

Resources: Filmstrips, slides, pictures, and readings on ancient Athens, wax, pencil, knife, and paper.

Activity: Students will read a selection about everyday life in ancient Athens. Since the Greeks were among the first to make cameos, have students examine a real cameo. Students will then look at filmstrips, slides, and pictures which show scenes similar to the reading. Students will then examine the pictures and draw a scene to be carved into a cameo of wax. Beforehand, the teacher will prepare wax to be carved. (In a pan, pour colored parafin. When it is almost hard, pour clear or white melted parafin. When solid, the block is ready to be carved into a cameo scene—Figure 34, page 140.) The student will draw the scene on the top of the solid clear or white wax and carve the scene.

Social Studies–Greece, Ancient (II) (cont'd)

Figure 34

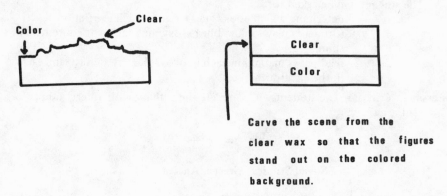

Carve the scene from the clear wax so that the figures stand out on the colored background.

Assessment Criteria: The student will complete the project with a picture related to the reading.

■ ■ ■

Social Studies–Holidays; Abraham Lincoln's Birthday, February 12

Media Skills Objectives: Use atlases

Use gazetteers

Level: 5-6

Learning Strategy: Practice

Performance Objective: Given an atlas and a gazetteer, the student will find twenty towns, cities, counties, lakes, and rivers which have been named after Abraham Lincoln.

Resources: Atlas, gazetteer, paper, and pencil.

Activity: After showing students how to use the atlas' index and the gazetteer, the student will find twenty places named Lincoln. (Note: A competition can be arranged by having students identify other place names derived from the names of famous people such as Washington or Jefferson.)

Students will identify the places and the latitude and longitude on their paper.

Example:

Lincoln, California	38·51 N	121·19 W
Lincoln, Illinois	40·09 N	89·21 W
Lincoln, Kansas	39·02 N	98·08 W
Lincoln, Maine	45·23 N	68·31 W

Assessment Criteria: Using an atlas or gazetteer, the student will identify twenty places and give the latitude and longitude of those places.

Social Studies—Holidays;
George Washington's Birthday, February 22

Media Skills Objectives: Identify and locate encyclopedias.

Select and distinguish among volumes of an alphabetically arranged encyclopedia to find information on a given topic.

Use an encyclopedia to locate information.

Level: 4

Learning Strategy: Individual/group project

Performance Objective: Given the assignment of finding George Washington's 110 boyhood rules of behavior, the student will find the proper volume of the encyclopedia and the rules George Washington prepared.

Resources: *The World Book Encyclopedia*, paper, and pencil.

Activity: After a discussion concerning the ways in which students today are required to behave in school and in the media center, the teacher will ask students if they think there has been any change in expected behavior since George Washington's time. The students need to know how children were required to behave in the eighteenth century. They will use George Washington as an example and look for information on his boyhood in the encyclopedia (*The World Book Encyclopedia*). When the appropriate article is found, students will be asked to write those rules of behavior which are the same and those which have changed somewhat. These rules may be placed on two large charts for purposes of comparison.

Assessment Criteria: The student will find the correct encyclopedia volume and article on George Washington and identify George Washington's boyhood rules of behavior. They will correctly separate rules which are the same as or different from current behavior standards.

■ ■ ■

Social Studies—Holidays;
Mother's Day, Second Sunday in May

Media Skills Objective: Identify and trace the development of a character (motivation).

Level: 2-4

Learning Strategy: Reading, discussion

Performance Objective: After reading four stories that involve mothers, the students will discuss characteristics and behavior of the mother in each story.

Resources: Four books such as:
Hill, Elizabeth Starr. *Evan's Corner*. Holt, Rinehart and Winston, 1967.
Seuss, Dr. *Horton Hatches the Egg*. Random House, 1940.
McCloskey, Robert. *Make Way for Ducklings*. Viking, 1941.
Kraus, Robert. *Leo the Late Bloomer*. Windmill Books, 1973.

Social Studies—Holidays;
Mother's Day, Second Sunday in May (cont'd)

Activity: The students will be given a chance to read the four books. In a small group (4-6 students), students will be asked to tell about the mother in each story. Students may be asked questions such as:

How did the mother in each story act toward her child?

What kinds of words describe each mother in the stories?

What kinds of things about each mother made you feel happy or angry?

What do you suppose made each mother act as she did?

How would you feel if each of the mothers was yours?

How would you feel if you were each of the mothers?

Which of the mothers in the stories would you most like to honor on Mother's Day? Why? Which would you least like to honor? Why?

Assessment Criteria: The student will give plausible answers to the questions.

■ ■ ■

Social Studies—Holidays;
Christmas, December 25

Media Skills Objective: Prepare notes using a simple organizational pattern.

Level: 5-8

Learning Strategy: Project, practice

Performance Objective: Given two written reports on the history of Christmas cards, which may be copied or adapted from encyclopedias or other reference sources, the student will take notes according to an organizational pattern given him.

Resources: Written discourse on the history of Christmas cards, organizational pattern, paper, and pencil.

Activity: Before the student is given two articles on Christmas cards, he will be shown a method of taking notes.

Guidelines for Notetaking:
1. Have a supply of 3x5-inch cards (cut paper).
2. Write each fact or idea on a separate card.
3. Use only abbreviations that will have meaning for you later.
4. In the top right hand corner, put the source of your information.
5. Give the page number on which the information was found.
6. On each note card, put the main idea first.
7. Under the main idea, put the specific facts or information related to the main idea.
8. Copy all quotes word-for-word.

When the students understand the process, give them two short articles on the history of Christmas cards. Students will take notes and then put the notes together in order to write one article.

Social Studies—Holidays; Christmas (cont'd)

Assessment Criteria: The student will produce at least three notecards from each article showing that the process was followed.

■ ■ ■

Social Studies—Indians, American (I)

Media Skills Objectives: Identify and locate records and record players.

Translate oral or written directions from a resource into a product or action.

Level: 2-5

Learning Strategy: Audiovisual instruction, practice

Performance Objective: The student will locate a record and instructions for performing an Indian dance, and a record player on which to play the music.

Resources: Records which have Indian dances and directions, such as *Music of American Indians*, RCA, or authentic music with instructions and a record player.

Activity: The teacher will give the following instructions:
1. Locate music used with either the
   a. Eagle Dance
   b. Snake Dance
   c. Dance for Rain
   d. Corn Dance
   e. Buffalo Hunt Dance
   f. Dance of the Medicine Men
   g. Indian Hoop Dance
2. Find a source that will explain steps of one of the dances.
3. Locate a record player.
4. Play the music.
5. Learn the dance.
6. Perform this dance for other members of your class.

Assessment Criteria: The student will locate a record, dance information, a record player, and learn the dance.

■ ■ ■

Social Studies—Indians, American (II)

Media Skills Objectives: Identify and locate encyclopedias.

Select an encyclopedia to find information on a given subject.

Interpret simple charts.

Use an encyclopedia to locate information.

Social Studies—Indians, American (II) (cont'd)

Level: 3-6

Learning Strategy: Practice

Performance Objective: Given a series of geographical living areas, homes, crafts and weapons of various American Indian tribes, the student will find the appropriate volume of the encyclopedia and use the chart to match the series of words.

Resources: *The World Book Encyclopedia*, worksheet of names to match, and pencil.

Activity: The student will use the *World Book Encyclopedia* to match the following:

Buildings	Area	Crafts and weapons
Navaho hogan	Plains	Snowshoe
Inca temple	Northwest coast	Salmon spear
Panoan house	Middle America	Toboggan
Pueblo	Tropical forest	Blowgun
Paiute brush wick	Southwest	Bow
Haida plank house	Caribbean	Digging stick
Sioux buffalo-hide	Andes	Fishhook
teepee	Far North	Water basket
Seminole house	Eastern woodlands	Gourd rattle
Kickapoo wigwam	California and	Grinding stone
	intermountain	Quipu
		Reed boat
		Wooden drums
		Bird snare
		Guanaco bola

Assessment Criteria: The student will correctly match the columns on both sides missing no more than seven items.

■ ■ ■

Social Studies—Indians, American (III)

Media Skills Objectives: Identify and locate dictionaries and encyclopedias.

Distinguish between a dictionary and an encyclopedia and select one for a particular purpose.

Find words in a dictionary.

Use a dictionary to find the meaning, part of speech, derivation, syllabication, and pronunciation of a word.

Use an encyclopedia to locate information.

Level: 3-6

Learning Strategy: Lecture, practice

Social Studies—Indians, American (III) (cont'd)

Performance Objective: Given a series of questions about totems and totem poles, the student will determine whether to use a dictionary or an encyclopedia and will find the answers to the questions.

Resources: Dictionary appropriate to level, encyclopedia, worksheet, and pencil.

Activity: Students will be instructed that they are to determine for themselves whether a dictionary or an encyclopedia is appropriate to answer specific questions after they have listened to a lecture about the differences between the two. The types of information found in each resource and the purpose of both will be reviewed with students, who will then be given the worksheet.

Worksheet:
Examine the following questions concerning totems or totem poles. Decide, after reading each problem, whether a dictionary or an encyclopedia would give the proper answer. Find the solution.

Problem	Source and Page	Answer
a. What is a totem or totem pole?		
b. What tribes make totem poles?		
c. What part of speech is "totem"?		
d. How is a totem pole made?		
e. How is the word "totem" divided into syllables?		
f. Is there more than one meaning for the word "totem"?		
g. Why were totem poles made?		
h. How do you use totem in a sentence?		
i. What did totem poles represent?		
j. Where is the accent mark on the word "totem"?		
k. How is the word "totem" pronounced?		

Assessment Criteria: The student will complete the assignment missing no more than four answers.

■ ■ ■

Social Studies—Maps

Media Skills Objective: Find directions on simple maps and globes.

Level: 3-6

Learning Strategy: Game, practice

Performance Objective: Given a game which requires the student to move in the four cardinal directions, the student will move in the direction identified and complete the game.

Social Studies—Maps (cont'd)

Resources: Game (teacher-prepared)

Activity: The teacher will explain the game to students. Four students may play. The object is to drive across town. Each player has a small car. There is a stack of cards which have the words: North, East, South, or West on them. There are more cards listing east or north. There are also small cards saying, "Drive to the school . . . shopping center . . . etc." Students, one at a time, spin the spinner which tells them to move their cars one, two, or three blocks. They must draw a card to tell in which direction. The roads follow standard map symbols which are located on the board (Figure 35). The first child to get across town wins.

Figure 35

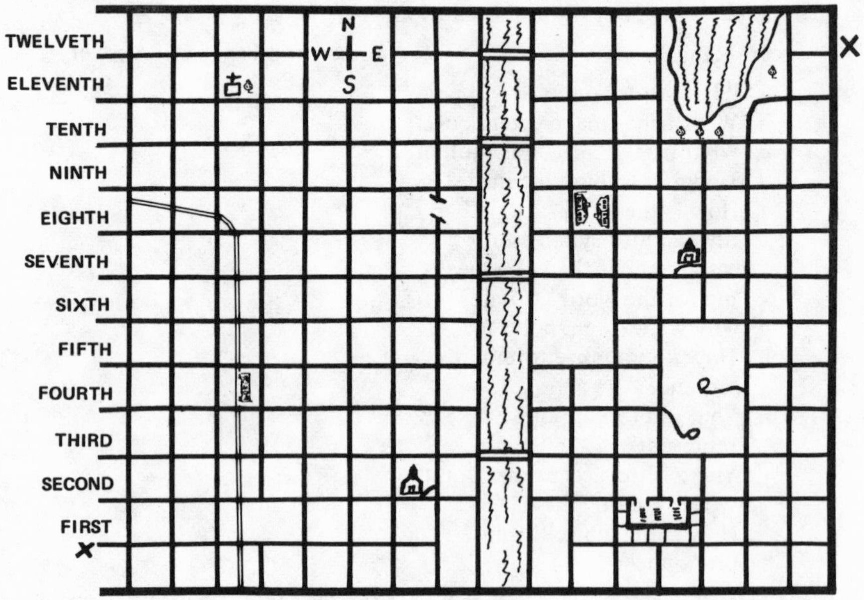

Assessment Criteria: The students playing will move their cars in the correct direction.

■ ■ ■

Social Studies–Prehistoric Life

Media Skills Objective: Interpret simple graphs and charts.

Level: 2-4

Learning Strategy: Learning center

Performance Objective: Given a graph showing the evolution of dinosaurs and prehistoric life, the student will identify specific specimens and tell how they may have evolved.

Resources: Chart of the dinosaur evolutionary family tree, plastic dinosaurs or pictures, set of questions and instructions.

Activity: Students will be given the set of prehistoric animals so that they can handle and look at them. When students have familiarized themselves with the animals, the instructor will discuss with the students how information on these animals has been accumulated and the fact that these animals did not all live at the same time. After being shown the starting point of the chronological chart, the students will arrange the figures on the chart chronologically and answer questions.

For example:
1. Which came first? Ankylosaurus or Brontosaurus
2. Would bones of the triceratops be older or younger than those of the stegosaurus?

Animals include:

Ankylosaurus
Triceratops
Diatryma
Moschops
Allosaurus
Styracosaurus
Smilodon
Stegosaurus
Wooly Mammoth
Pteranodon
Macrauchenia
Ceratogaulus
Cynognaphis
Parasaurolophus
Megatherium
Dire Wolf

Assessment Criteria: The student will put the animals in correct order, missing only one, and will answer the questions correctly.

■ ■ ■

Social Studies—School

Media Skills Objective: Locate material and information using a sample map.

Level: 2-4

Learning Strategy: Lecture, practice

Performance Objective: Given a large but simple map of the school and homes around the school, the student will use it to find the shortest, longest, quickest, and safest way from home to school.

Resources: One large school community map, plastic, grease pencil.

Activity: A simple map of the community should be prepared, which includes the school and homes of children involved in the activity. Have a large plastic sheet which may be placed over the community map and written upon. Children will find their home on the map (they must know their addresses). They will find the school. With the plastic sheet covering the map, students will draw four lines of different colors showing:
1. the shortest way
2. the longest way
3. the safest way
4. the quickest way

If they come to school by bus, students may need some assistance.

Assessment Criteria: The student will accurately draw at least three of the four routes.

■ ■ ■

Social Studies—United States Geography

Media Skills Objectives: Identify and locate: records, record players, cassettes, cassette tape recorder, filmstrips, filmstrip previewers, filmloops, filmloop projectors, the non-fiction collection, slides, slide previewers, the card catalog, book catalogs, the vertical file, periodicals, newspapers, transparencies, overhead projectors, encyclopedias, tapes, tape recorders, pamphlets, clippings, indexes, maps and globes, guide to children's periodicals, almanacs, atlases, films, and film projectors.

Identify and locate a title page, the table of contents, an illustration list, a map list, and an index in a print item.

Locate a specific item of information in a title page, a table of contents, a map list, an illustration list, a simple map, and an index.

Locate specific sources in the card catalog by author, title, or subject.

Locate a specific resource in the media center using the call number of the item given on a catalog card.

Locate specific information about an item on the catalog card.

Identify and locate materials using the *Dewey Decimal System of Classification.*

Social Studies—United States Geography (cont'd)

Media Skills Objectives (cont'd)

Select the appropriate sources and necessary instructional equipment given specific topics.

Select a reference source based on knowledge of its purpose.

Operate a record player, a cassette tape recorder, a listening station, a filmstrip previewer, an 8mm filmloop projector, a slide previewer, an overhead projector, a reel-to-reel tape recorder, and a film projector.

Use a telephone directory.

Use sections of a newspaper and its indexes to locate specific information for a definite purpose.

Find directions on simple maps and globes.

Interpret simple maps, globes, graphs, and charts.

Find specific information in materials using guide words, headings, subheadings, key words, phrases, and topic sentences.

Skim materials to find a word, name, date, phrase, sentence, idea, or answer to a question.

Paraphrase simple information.

Use a map key to obtain information and a map scale to compute distance.

Use an encyclopedia to locate information or solve a problem.

Identify alternate topics using cross references.

Use almanacs, atlases, gazetteers, simple guides to children's periodicals, special dictionaries, and special indexes.

Summarize simple information found in resources.

Generalize information found in resources.

Compare facts, ideas, and visual images from more than one source.

Draw conclusions on a given topic from more than one source.

Level: 5-8

Learning Strategy: Project

Performance Objective: Given a project booklet with specific activities involving a trip to a given state, the student will complete all the activities correctly in accordance with the directions specified in each activity.

Resources: Media Center collection, road maps, motel books, booklet, and pencil.

Activity: This is a six-week unit. It focuses on location skills but incorporates others as well. It can be prepared by the student in the form of a booklet.

Students will need a great deal of individual help and instruction along the way, and should be given an introduction to most of the necessary skills beforehand. Since the activity is a project, points have been assigned to each part. It may be divided into segments and made into a project learning center. Students will be allowed to select their own state. The finished product will take the form of a booklet.

Social Studies—United States Geography (cont'd)

Activity (cont'd)

Two-Week State Vacation Project

You are going to take an imaginary trip to the state of
_____ . It will last two weeks. You are to
use the resources in the Media Center and other materials to take this
trip.

Part I (worth 25 points)

First, you must identify areas of interest in your chosen state. You will look
for the following areas in your state and write about them:

A.   Identify at least three historic places of interest. Write a paragraph
about each place and cite the resource you used to learn about it.
1.   Place: _____

_____

_____

_____

Source: (author)_____, _____(title)_____,
____(publisher)_____, _____(date)___, ___(page)___.
2.   Place: _____

_____

_____

_____

Source: _____, _____,
_____, _____, _____.
3.   Place: _____

_____

_____

_____

Source: _____, _____,
_____, _____, _____.

B.   Identify at least three places of natural wonder. Write a paragraph
about each place and cite the resource you used to learn about it.
1.   Place: _____

_____

_____

_____

Source: _____, _____,
_____, _____, _____.
2.   Place: _____

_____

_____

_____

Source: _____, _____,
_____, _____, _____.

Social Studies–United States Geography (cont'd)

Activity (cont'd)

3. Place:_____
   _____
   _____
   _____

   Source: _____ , _____ ,
   _____ , _____ , _____ .

C. Identify at least one agricultural product of your state and in what part of the state it is produced. Cite the material you used to find this information.
   Product: _____
   Part of State: _____
   Source: _____ , _____ ,
   _____ , _____ , _____ .

D. Find material which gives you a visual image of what your state is like. Find at least 10 pictures and cite your sources.

E. Watch the newspaper for one week to see if you can find out some of the activities which may be going on in your chosen state. Cite the source.

(Suggested Search Pattern for Part I)

1. Think of several key words which you might use to identify your state, e.g., your state's name or geographic region. What things do you already know about the state? List those things.

2. Look for information using the key words you have identified in the following places:

   Card Catalog for:
       books (use index in specific books)
       records
       maps and globes
       filmstrips
       tapes
       charts
       pictures
       filmloops
       transparencies
       films
   Encyclopedias
   Magazines
       National Geographic Index
       Subject Guide to Children's Periodicals
       Abridged Reader's Guide to Periodicals
   Vertical File
   Telephone Directory
   Public Library Catalog

Social Studies—United States Geography (cont'd)

Activity (cont'd)

Part II (worth 25 points)

A.   Now that you know some of the places of interest in your state, obtain a road map.

B.   Mark places on the map which you would like to visit. Consult **Part I** above.

C.   Determine the best routes to each place and the order in which you will visit various places. (Use the better roads and the most direct routes.)

D.   Using the scale, determine the distance between each place and how long it will take to get from each place to the next. (Drive under the speed limit: 50 miles per hour average.)

E.   Plan your itinerary day by day, including where you will visit, how long it will take to get there, roads you will take, where you will spend the night, eat, and stop for rest. (You may stay at a motel, camp out, stay with relatives, etc.)

Figure 36

Day	Place Visited	Roads

Part III (worth 25 points)

A.   Now that you know where you'll be going, estimate how much the trip will cost.

    1.   Gas
(Check how much gasoline costs per gallon and add up the number of miles you will be traveling. Find out what kind of car you have and its mileage. Determine how many gallons it will take and multiply by the cost per gallon.)

    2.   Food
(Use the newspaper to check food prices if you are camping out. Add up the number of meals you'll be eating. Call some restaurants to find an estimate of what it might cost to eat out.)

    3.   Lodging
(Find out from motel guides how much it might cost to stay in a motel. Or, find out how much it might cost to stay in a campground. If you camp out, include the cost of your equipment.)

    4.   Miscellaneous
(Sometimes there is an admission fee to attractions. You might wish to buy souvenirs, film, etc.)

B.   Add all of these costs and that will be an estimate for your trip.

Social Studies—United States Geography (cont'd)

Activity (cont'd)

Part IV (worth 25 points)

Make a diary of your trip and the experiences you might have. It can be done in writing, with pictures, or on a tape. It should be a day-by-day record. Include humorous incidents which might have occurred.

Assessment Criteria: The student will complete the project earning no less than 60 points.

■ ■ ■

Social Studies—United States History, Westward Movement

Media Skills Objectives: Identify and locate specific reference materials.

Select the appropriate sources and necessary instructional equipment given specific topics.

Use more than one source to gather information.

Use lines, colors, shapes, and textures to create symbols.

Level: 6-8

Learning Strategy: Project

Performance Objective: Given a specific topic on the Westward Movement (after 1860s) and resources, the student will select and use appropriate resources in order to design and prepare a tissue paper tiffany lamp.

Resources: Print and nonprint materials related to the Westward Movement, paper, construction paper, colored tissue paper, glue, scissors, coat hangers (wire), wire cutters, X-acto knife, and pencils.

Activity: The students will make tiffany lamp replicas from paper. They will be told that their designs are to be related to the Westward Movement after the Civil War. Each student will be assigned a specific topic such as:

> Forms of Transportation
> Hardships
> Styles and Dress
> Farm Life
> School and Education
> Homes
> Social Life

The students will then do the following:

1. Identify key words which will be employed in the use of references.
2. Identify and locate reference sources (print and nonprint).
3. Use the sources to identify relevant information (visual and printed).
4. Prepare six designs to represent their assigned topics.

Social Studies—United States History,
Westward Movement (cont'd)

Activity (cont'd)

 5. The designs will be placed on a lamp shaped in the following manner (Figure 37):

Figure 37

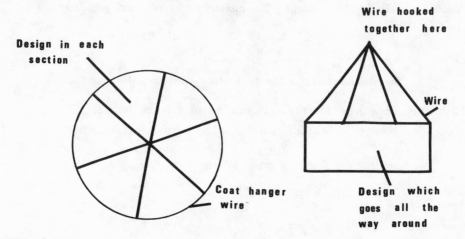

Designs will be cut from black construction paper to fit each section. (Note: Students should be told to make their designs simple and representative.) Pieces of colored tissue will be glued on the back of the design so that the light shines through the paper.

 6. Hang finished products around the room from the ceiling.

Students will explain their designs and topics.

Assessment Criteria: The student will identify more than one source of information on his assigned topic and will prepare a replica lamp with designs representing his topic.

■ ■ ■

Social Studies—Urban Life (I)

Media Skills Objective: Find specific information using picture clues in decoding.

Level: 1-3

Learning Strategy: Discussion

Performance Objective: Given a set of contrasting pictures of city slums and well-kept areas, the student will identify differences in the pictures and tell the characteristics of both.

Social Studies—Urban Life (I) (cont'd)

Resources: Set of pictures showing well-kept areas and buildings and areas which have not been well-kept. (These may be cut from magazines and mounted.)

Activity: The teacher will set up five pictures each of both kinds of neighborhoods. These pictures will be interspaced. The teacher or media specialist will first direct questions at identifying specific information in the pictures. Students may then identify obvious differences and discuss what makes some places "slums" while other places are not.

Assessment Criteria: The student will view the pictures and identify the differences, making at least one contribution to the discussion.

■ ■ ■

Social Studies—Urban Life (II)

Media Skills Objectives: Identify and locate tapes (reel).

Identify and locate tape recorders (reel-to-reel).

Select and match a reel tape with a reel-to-reel tape recorder to play or record audio information.

Operate a reel-to-reel tape recorder.

Prepare a reel-to-reel tape recording.

Level: 5-6

Learning Strategy: Demonstration, practice

Performance Objective: Given a tape recorder and access to various people who have lived in a specific urban area for a long time, the student will use the tape recorder to record an oral history interview.

Resources: Persons to interview, tape recorder, and reel-to-reel tape.

Activity: After a brief review of the operation of a tape recorder, students will identify areas of interest in urban life which they would like to explore through interviews. These areas might include:

      Government Figures
      Recreation
      Land Use
      Technology
      Transportation
      Social Life
      Family Life
      Dress
      Language and Slang

When specific subject areas have been determined, the student will prepare a set of questions to be asked of the interviewee. After questions have been prepared, the student is ready to tape an interview using a reel-to-reel tape recorder. Steps which the student will follow in using the tape recorder include:

Social Studies—Urban Life (II)

Activity (cont'd)

1. Connect the power cord and remove the cover.
2. Identify the correct threading path and thread the blank tape through the machine.
3. Connect the microphone.
4. Place the machine in the record mode.
5. Test the volume.
6. Rewind the tape recorder and make sure the machine is correctly threaded.
7. Set the counter.
8. Begin the tape in the record mode.
9. Tape the interview.
10. Stop the machine and rewind.
11. Replay the tape in the play mode.
12. Rewind the tape.
13. Turn off the machine.
14. Unplug the tape recorder and cover the machine.

Assessment Criteria: The student will use the tape recorder following demonstrated procedures and will tape an oral history interview.

■　■　■

Social Studies—Urban Life (III)

Media Skills Objectives: Support a main idea using facts found in a specified reference source.

Use footnotes to document information from resources.

Organize information to show sequence.

Level: 6-8.

Learning Strategy: Project

Performance Objective: Given resources on the immigration of people to a given metropolitan area, the student will find facts on the immigration of people to that city from a reference source, document each fact, and organize those facts into a sequence.

Resources: A reference work (one which deals historically with the immigration of people into a large metropolitan area, such as New York City), paper, printed style sheet to use for footnotes, and pencil.

Activity: The student will be given a project requiring the preparation of a "recipe" for the growth of a given city. Students will be informed that they are examining the history of the city and the immigration of various people to that city. Before they begin, they should identify some "recipe" terminology such as the following words: blend, mix, stir, whip, drop, measure, add, etc. Students will identify the groups of people who came to the city at various times in the city's history. A recipe in chronological order

Social Studies—Urban Life (III) (cont'd)

Activity (cont'd)

illustrating the immigration of people to the city will be prepared. Each "ingredient" is to be documented with a footnote in the following form:

> Name of Author, *Title of Book*, Translator or Editor, Name of Series and Volume, Place of Publication, Publisher, Date, Volume and Page Numbers.

Assessment Criteria: The student will use a specified reference work and identify the major groups of people who immigrated into a given city. The facts will be organized in correct chronological sequence in the form of a recipe and will be documented in the specified form.

■ ■ ■

Social Studies—World Communities

Media Skills Objectives: Identify and locate almanacs.

Use almanacs.

Level: 3-6

Learning Strategy: Practice

Performance Objective: Given a series of flags from various countries and the information that flags may be found in the *World Almanac*, the student will locate the almanac, find the correct pages on which flags may be found, and identify the country to which each flag belongs.

Resources: *The World Almanac*, worksheet of world flags, pencil.

Activity: Students will be introduced to the idea that flags or banners stand for something or mean special things. The flags on the worksheet stand for specific countries.

Worksheet:
Use *The World Almanac* or another almanac to fill in the names of the proper countries to which these flags belong (Figure 38). It may help you to color the flags first.

Figure 38

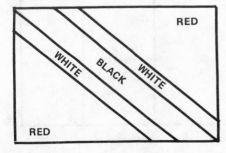
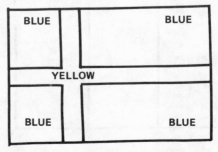

Social Studies—World Communities (cont'd)

Activity (cont'd)

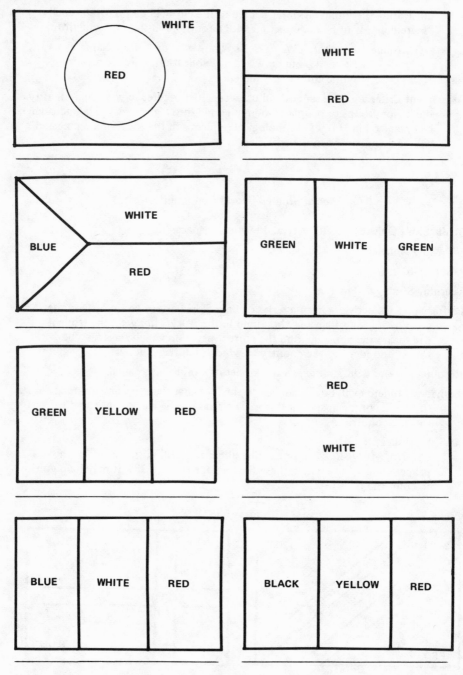

Social Studies—World Communities (cont'd)

Assessment Criteria: The student will identify all flags with no mistakes.

Answers:

Trinidad	Sweden
Japan	Poland
Czechoslovakia	Nigeria
Mali	Monaco
France	Belgium

PART III—BIBLIOGRAPHY OF
INSTRUCTIONAL MATERIALS FOR
MEDIA SKILLS

INTRODUCTION

All of the activities and lessons suggested in Parts I and II may be undertaken without the use of commercial materials designed to teach library, communication, and media skills. Nevertheless, such materials are abundantly available and may, in certain lessons, serve as valuable supplements to lessons and materials prepared by teachers and media specialists. The following bibliography is not by any means exhaustive, but it includes many of the better materials currently available in a wide range of formats. Prices listed are current as of the publication date of this book but are subject to change.

NON-PRINT

Charts

Dictionary Skill Charts. Oak Lawn, Ill., Ideal School Supply, 1967.
  $11.00
  Grade level: 3-5
  Charts provide examples derived from many popular classroom dictionaries.

Encyclopedias: Their Similarities and Differences. Bronx, N.Y., Fordham Equipment and Publishing Co., 1969.
  $ 7.50
  Grade level: 6-
  A large laminated chart gives information about six adult encyclopedias and two one-volume editions.

Enlarged Wilson Catalog Cards. Sturgis, Mich., Sturgis Library Products, undated.
  $15.00
  Grade level: 3-
  Thirty-two enlarged examples of author, title, subject, and shelf list cards. (Various sets available.)

How to Find a Book. Syracuse, N.Y., Gaylord, undated.
  $ 1.00
  Grade level: 3-8
  Poster illustrates Dewey Decimal main classes and provides descriptions and examples of each class.

How to Find a Book. Williamsport, Pa., Bro-Dart, undated.
$ 1.00
Grade level: 3-8
Poster illustrates Dewey Decimal main classes and provides descriptions and examples of each class.

How to Read Maps. Chicago, Field Enterprises Educational Corporation, 1966.
$ 0.25
Grade level: 3-7
Enlargement from *World Book Encyclopedia.*

How to Use the Card Catalog. Birmingham, Ala., Nifty Division, St. Regis Paper Co.
$10.95
Grade level: 3-6
Twelve large charts (24x36-inch) give simple information on basic card catalog facts.

Library Skill Charts. Oak Lawn, Ill., Ideal School Supply, 1967.
$11.00
Grade level: 3-6
Eighteen charts (23x36-inch) with teacher's manual illustrate very basic library skill information dealing with location and organization of materials.

Map Symbols and Geographic Terms. Chicago, Nystrom, 1967.
$63.50
Grade level: 3-7
Detailed charts related to the use of map and geographic terminology.

Using Your Library. Duluth, Minn., F. A. Owen, Instructor Publications, 1974.
$ 7.50
Grade level: 3-6
Thirty-two charts (13x16-inch) with guide usable for library orientation, selection skills, the card catalog, and writing reports.

Vicalog: Eye-Gate Visual Card Catalog. Jamaica, N.Y., Eye-Gate, undated.
$ 7.50
Grade level: 3-8
Chart of a catalog card (8½x14-inch) which may be converted into an author, title, or subject card with four acetate overlays.

What a Dictionary Tells You. Chicago, Field Enterprises Educational Corporation, 1966.
$ 0.25
Grade level: 4-7
An enlargement of an entry from a dictionary with each information item labeled.

Filmstrips

Beginning Dictionary Skills. Los Angeles, Audio-Education, Inc., 1963.
$24.00
Grade level: 3-5
Titles include: *Finding Entry Words, Understanding Entries, Pronouncing Words Correctly,* and *Using What You Know.*

Four color strips with cartoon drawings introduce basic dictionary skills, such as arrangement and location of words, using *Webster's Beginning Dictionary.*

The Dictionary in Action. Huntsville, Tex., Educational Filmstrips, 1962.
$18.00
Grade level: 5-9
Titles include: Part 1, Part 2, and Part 3

Reinforces the use of the dictionary in spelling, syllabication, accents, parts of speech, plurals, capitalization, etymology, illustrations, and multiple meanings.

Extending Dictionary Skills. Los Angeles, Audio-Education, Inc., 1963.
$24.00
Grade level: 6-9
Titles include: *Using the Complete Entry, Finding and Using Exact Meanings, Understanding Parts of Speech,* and *Putting Dictionary Skills to Work.*

Strips for secondary students with cartoon-colored drawings using *Webster's Secondary School Dictionary.*

Fun in the City: Libraries. New York, McGraw-Hill, 1968.
$ 7.75
Grade level: 2-4
Introduction to the card catalog and check-out procedures, with particular reference to local public libraries.

How the Card Catalog Helps You. El Cerrito, Calif., Long Filmslide Service, 1968.
$20.00
Grade level: 3-5
Titles include: *Parts of the Catalog Card, Author Cards, Title Cards,* and *Subject Cards.*

This filmstrip set is particularly helpful because it includes separate strips on subject, author, and title.

Library Services Series. Jamaica, N.Y., Eye-Gate, 1963.
    $28.00
    Grade level: 2-6
    Titles include: *Explaining the Dewey Decimal Classification, Introduction to the Card Catalog, Parts of a Book,* and *Using Reference Materials.*

Filmstrip series illustrates basic media skills.

Library Research Tools Series. Jamaica, N.Y., Eye-Gate, 1964.
    $70.00
    Grade level: 5-9
    Titles include: *Introduction to the Library, The Book, The Card Catalog, Dictionaries, Encyclopedias, Selected References–General, Selected References–Specific, Periodical References and Indices, The Research Paper: Preliminary Stages,* and *The Research Paper: Bibliography and Footnotes.*

Filmstrip set presents an overview of research techniques and reference sources. The filmstrips on *The Book* and *Encyclopedias* are especially useful.

Library Tools Series. New York, McGraw-Hill, 1959.
    $44.00
    Grade level: 5-8
    Titles include: *One Volume Encyclopedias, Books for Biography, Reader's Guide to Periodical Literature, Gazetteers and Atlases, Aids in Writing and Reading,* and *Almanacs and Yearbooks.*

Captioned filmstrips give very usable information in each subject as shown in the titles.

Look It Up! New York, Filmstrip House, 1962.
    $20.00
    Grade level: 7-
    Titles include: *Discovering the Dictionary; Finding Facts and Figures; Periodicals, Biographies, and Quotations;* and *Pinpointing What You Want.*

Intermediate information on subjects indicated by the titles. Format somewhat outdated, but contents are accurate and useful.

Looking Up Facts and Information. Mahwah, N.J., Troll, 1970.
    $ 7.00
    Grade level: 3-7
    Excellent treatment of the use of the card catalog and shelf arrangement.

Map and Globe Series: Using Globes; Set 1. New York, McGraw-Hill, 1968.
$43.50
Grade level: 3-6
Titles include: *Learning about Continents and Oceans, Learning about North and South, Learning about East and West, Learning How to Find Direction, Learning about Rotation,* and *Learning How to Use the Sun to Find Direction.*

Detailed series of filmstrips on every aspect of maps and globes. Set 1 provides introductory material.

Map and Globe Series: Using Maps; Set 2. New York, McGraw-Hill, 1968.
$65.00
Grade level: 3-6
Titles include: *Introduction to Maps, Making a Floor Plan, Scale, Measuring Distances, Locating Places, Where on Earth Do You Live?, Map Symbols, Land-Water Features,* and *Special Maps.*

Detailed series of filmstrips on every aspect of maps and globes. Set 2 relates maps to the study of elementary geography.

The School Library Series. New York, McGraw-Hill, 1965.
$49.00
Grade level: 5-8
Titles include: *Using Books; The Dewey Decimal System; The Card Catalog; The Dictionary, Part I; The Dictionary, Part II;* and *The Encyclopedia.*

Introductory material on subjects specified in each title.

Taking a Trip with a Book. Mahwah, N.J., Troll, 1968.
$ 7.00
Grade level: K-2
Simple filmstrip provides an introduction to the functions of a library.

Using Books Efficiently. Berkeley, Calif., Pacific Productions, 1960.
$30.00
Grade level: 3-7
Titles include: *Choosing Books, Locating Facts in Books, Using Study Helps in Books,* and *Using the Card Catalog.*

Using Reference Materials. Mahwah, N.J., Troll, 1970.
$ 7.00
Grade level: 3-6
The useful functions of various reference books are presented to students.

Using the Library. Chicago, Encyclopaedia Britannica, 1963.
$39.00
Grade level: 4-8
Titles include: *Your Library, a World of Books*; *The Card Catalog*; *The Classification of Books*; *Using the Dictionary*; *Using the Encyclopedia*; *Using Special Reference Books.*

Set provides an overview of library services and skills.

A Visit to the Library. Mahwah, N.J., Troll, 1969.
$ 7.00
Grade level: K-2
Librarian gives a tour of the library emphasizing the card catalog and book arrangement.

Games, Instructional Materials

Alphabetical Order. Paoli, Pa., Instructo, 1974.
$ 7.95
Grade level: 1-4
Learning game board, cards, cubes and spirit masters in a carnival motif teach students alphabetical order.

Care for Books. New York, Children's Book Council.
$ 2.50 per 100
Grade level: K-3
The bookmarks, drawn by Hardy Gramatky, illustrate the care and protection of books.

Dewey Blocks. Bronx, N.Y., Fordham Equipment and Publishing Co., 1973.
$32.95
Grade level: 1-6
Manual and large blocks for each main Dewey Decimal Classification number provide activities which help students understand this system of arrangement.

Fact and Opinion. Paoli, Pa., Instructo, 1975.
$ 5.95
Grade level: 4-6
A learning center kit comprised of games and puzzles which provides instruction in distinguishing fact from fiction.

How a Book Is Made. New York, Children's Book Council.
$ 2.50 per 100
Grade level: 4-7
Bookmarks designed by Leonard Kessler illustrate the process of book making.

How to Find a Book Bookmarks. Sturgis, Mich., Sturgis.
$ 5.75 per 500
Grade level: 3-6
Bookmarks illustrate each of the main Dewey Decimal classes.

Story Sequence. Paoli, Pa., Instructo, 1975.
$ 5.95
Grade level: 1-3
Puzzles and other activities in the learning center kit reinforce student skills
in story sequences.

Kits

Biography, Background for Inspiration. Wichita, Kans., Library Filmstrip Center,
1967.
$23.00
Grade level: 7-
The thirteen-minute sound filmstrip provides an overview of the location
of biographical information.

The Card Catalog. Wichita, Kans., Library Filmstrip Center, 1968.
$23.00
Grade level: 6-
This fourteen-minute sound filmstrip presents the specific rules of using the
card catalog, including filing, cross-references, added entries, etc.

Exploring the World of Maps. Washington, D.C., National Geographic Society,
1973.
$67.50
Grade level: 5-9
Five sound filmstrips explain map symbols, scales, distances, directions, and
map production.

Getting Your Wordsworth: A Multimedia Kit. Englewood Cliffs, N.J., Prentice-
Hall, 1972.
$29.95
Grade level: 6-
Multimedia kit introducing the history and philosophy of the dictionary as
well as basic dictionary skills.

Graph and Practice Skills Kit. Chicago, Science Research Associates, 1970.
$160.00
Grade level: 4-8
Programmed texts help students identify and use graphs, charts, diagrams,
and other graphic materials.

Information Fast! Inglewood, Calif., Educational Insights, 1974.
$ 5.95
Grade level: 4-9
Ten sets of 125 activities for reinforcement in library and research skills.

An Introduction to the Library. Pleasantville, N.Y., Schloat, 1970.
$70.00
Grade level: 4-8
Four sound filmstrips orient students to particular aspects of the library collection, with emphasis on location of materials in specific subject areas.

Libraries Are for Children. Bronx, N.Y., Fordham Equipment and Publishing Co., 1968.
$159.50
Grade level: 3-7
The kit introduces arrangement of materials, types of materials, the Dewey Decimal System, card catalog, and comparison of encyclopedias.

Library Media Center Series. New York, ACI Films, 1973.
$82.00
Grade level: 3-8
Titles include: *Using Books in the Library Media Center, Introduction to the Library Media Center, Exploring the Card Catalog, Using Reference Tools— The Encyclopedia and the Dictionary*, and *Using Audiovisual Materials in the Library Media Center.*

Five sound filmstrips with guide.

The Library: Our Learning Resource Center—Set 2. New York, McGraw-Hill, 1975.
$72.00
Grade level: 3-6
Titles include: *Gazetteers and Atlases, Almanacs and Yearbooks, Dictionary*, and *Encyclopedias.*

Content is simply presented with follow-up activities in the guide.

The Library: Our Learning Resource Center—Set 3. New York, McGraw-Hill, 1975.
$72.00
Grade level: 4-6
Titles include: *A-V Materials and Equipment, How to Use and Care for Learning Resources, Periodical Indexes*, and *Doing Research.*

The strips introduce the care and use of materials as well as research, using two bookworms as guides. A brief guide-sheet is included.

Literature for Children—Series One. Verdugo, Calif., Pied Piper, 1971.
$62.50
Grade level: 4-6
Titles include: *Story of a Book*, *Biography*, *Tall Tales*, and *Fantasy*.

Audiovisual book-talks and author presentations illustrate topics indicated in individual filmstrip titles.

Literature for Children—Series Two. Verdugo, Calif., Pied Piper, 1971.
$62.50
Grade level: 4-6
Titles include: *Animals*, *Distant Lands*, *Fairy Tales*, and *Humor*.

Each strip presents an episode on the given topic with a review at the conclusion of each strip.

Literature for Children—Series Three. Verdugo, Calif., Pied Piper, 1971.
$62.50
Grade level: 4-6
Titles include: *Enjoying Illustrations*, *Myths*, *Historical Fiction*, and *Adventure*.

Four visual book-talks present titles in each subject area with some instruction in media skills.

Media for Moppets. Hueytown, Ala., Educational Services, 1969.
$72.00
Grade level: K-3
Titles include: *Learn-Look-Listen*, *Moppets' Media Manners*, *How to Use Media*, *Which Books to Use*, *Look*, and *Listen*.

Elementary orientation to the contents and use of the media center.

Map and Globe Skills Development Kit. Westchester, Ill., Benefic Press.
$98.95
Grade level: 4-6
Programmed kit including books, transparencies, and workbooks designed to teach basic map skills.

Map and Globe Skills Kit. Chicago, Science Research Associates, 1964.
$167.00
Grade level: 4-8
This programmed set provides students with help in map and globe skills.

Media: Resources for Discovery. Chicago, Encyclopaedia Britannica Educational Corporation, 1974.
$128.00
Grade level: 5-7
Titles include: *Resources for Reference*, *Choosing the Medium*, *Indexes to*

Media, *World of Media*, *One Search*, *One Report*, *Encyclopedia*, *Media Organization—Fiction*, and *Media Organization—Non-Fiction*.

Multimedia Center. Wichita, Kans., Library Filmstrip Center, 1970.
$23.00
Grade level: 5-
Intermediate survey of the contents of a media center, both print and non-print.

Newslab. Chicago, Science Research Associates, 1972.
$75.00
Grade level: 4-8
Through programmed cards, students practice skills necessary for use of the newspaper.

Newslab II. Chicago, Science Research Associates, 1975.
$75.00
Grade level: 5-9
Within specific subject areas, students receive detailed instruction in the use of a newspaper.

Organizing and Reporting Skills Kit. Chicago, Science Research Associates, 1970.
$160.00
Grade level: 5-9
Research skills necessary for preparing reports are the focal point of the programmed skills kit.

Reading, Researching and Reporting in Social Studies: Americana. Santa Monica, Calif., BFA, 1974.
$111.00
Grade level: 5-7
Four sound filmstrips, spirit masters, eight books, fifty activity cards, and a teacher's guide teach research and study skills specifically related to Social Studies.

Reference Resources Skills Development Kit. Westchester, Ill., Benefic Press.
$102.00
Grade level: 4-8
Student books, transparencies, and spirit masters provide practice in basic library skills.

Researchlab. Chicago, Science Research Associates, 1974.
$120.67
Grade level: 4-8
Two hundred and twenty cards provide research practice in reference tools, encyclopedias, and media skills for ten specific subject areas.

Using Maps and Globes. Chicago, Denoyer-Geppert, 1974.
$110.00
Grade level: 3-6
Titles include: *How to Use Maps, How to Use Globes,* and *How Earth Moves.*

Each set includes one sound filmstrip, a teacher's guide, and thirty student books with criterion-referenced tests. Concepts are developed through puppet illustrations.

Using the Elementary School Library. Chicago, Society of Visual Education, 1968.
$65.50
Grade level: 4-8
Titles include: *Skills in Gathering Facts, What's in the Dictionary, Getting to Know Books, How to Use the Card Catalog, How to Use the Encyclopedia,* and *Exploring the Library.*

Print and non-print media are introduced through well-organized media skills lessons.

Your Library—Place of Learning. Wichita, Kans., Library Filmstrip Center, 1967.
$23.00
Grade level: 6-
Audiovisual and print materials are discussed in relation to specific study skills.

Your Library Resources and How to Use the Readers' Guide. Bronx, N.Y., H. W. Wilson, 1973.
$95.00
Grade level: 7-
A sound filmstrip, three cassettes, and six transparencies with guides give detailed instructions for using the *Readers' Guide to Periodical Literature.*

Tapes

Dewey Decimal System No. 1. St. Paul, Minn., Wollensak, 1971.
$ 9.95
Grade level: 5-8
Worksheet exercises introduce the Dewey Decimal System in relation to particular subject areas, including practice in classifying non-fiction books.

Dewey Decimal System No. 2. St. Paul, Minn., Wollensak, 1971.
$ 9.95
Grade level: 6-
Exercises in Dewey Decimal Classification, illustrating subdivision to one digit beyond the decimal point, with examples in the numbers between 974 and 979.8.

Dictionary Skills. St. Paul, Minn., Wollensak, 1970.
$23.00
Grade level: 4-7
Worksheets on dictionary skills, incorporating practice in locating words, definitions, and the use of pronunciation keys.

Library Skills. Hamden, Conn., Learning Systems Corporation, 1969.
$69.00
Grade level: 3-6
Seven cassette tapes and student worksheets introduce topics in media skills including the Dewey Decimal System, location of fiction, the card catalog, and print and non-print media.

Reference Books No. 1. St. Paul, Minn., Wollensak, 1971.
$ 9.95
Grade level: 6-
Introduction to basic reference sources, including encyclopedias, yearbooks, almanacs, and atlases.

Reference Books No. 2. St. Paul, Minn., Wollensak, 1971.
$ 9.95
Grade level: 6-
Introduction to the use of the *Readers' Guide to Periodical Literature.*

Study Skills. Terry the Terrible Troll Series. Baltimore, Md., Media Materials, Inc., 1973.
$99.95 or $9.95 each
Grade level: 4-6
Titles include: *Terry the Terrible Dictates Directions, Terry the Terrible Tries the Table of Contents, Terry the Terrible Scrambles the Alphabet, Terry the Terrible Puts Troll Hill on the Map, Terry the Terrible's Picture Dictionary, Terry the Terrible Charts How He Grew, Terry the Terrible Graphs His Temper Tantrums, Terry the Terrible Indicates the Index, Terry the Terrible Sorts His Tools,* and *Terry the Terrible Troll Outlines His Life Story.*

Transparencies

Advanced Library Reference Skills. Chicago, Encyclopaedia Britannica Corporation, 1969.
$64.50
Grade level: 6-
This follow-up to *Library Reference Skills* provides an introduction to more complicated skills involving the card catalog, encyclopedias, etc.

Basic Dictionary Skills. St. Louis, Mo., Milliken, 1973.
> $ 7.95
> Grade level: 3-6
> Set of twenty-four spirit masters and twelve color transparencies provides
> the teacher with a guide to teaching dictionary skills and includes practice
> work for reinforcement of those skills.

Basic Library Skills. St. Louis, Mo., Milliken, 1971.
> $ 7.95
> Grade level: 3-7
> The twenty-four spirit masters and twelve color transparencies are sequen-
> tially arranged to provide an audiovisual introduction and an applicable
> practice activity for follow-up in such media skills as Dewey Decimal
> arrangement, alphabetizing, the card catalog, indexes, encyclopedias, and
> reference books.

Developing Questioning Skills. Redwood City, Calif., Visual Materials, Inc., 1970.
> $ 6.95
> Grade level: 5-
> Illustrates the development of good questions and questioning strategies.

The Encyclopedia. Atlanta, Ga., Colonial Films, 1967.
> $38.00
> Grade level: 4-8
> Set of transparencies contrasting the differences between dictionaries and
> encyclopedias.

Learning "Look-It-Up" Skills with a Dictionary. Chicago, Field Enterprises Educational Corporation, 1966.
> $ 6.95
> Grade level: 3-6
> Illustrates elementary dictionary skills.

Learning "Look-It-Up" Skills with an Encyclopedia. Chicago, Field Enterprises
Educational Corporation, 1966.
> $ 6.95
> Grade level: 3-6
> Simple-to-use transparencies introduce basic skills in the use of encyclopedias.

Library Instruction. Hoyoke, Maine, Scott Education Division, 1966.
> $90.00
> Grade level: 2-8
> Twenty-six transparencies help teach specific library skills such as how to
> check out materials, parts of a book, call numbers, and the card catalog.

Library Reference Skills. Chicago, Encyclopaedia Britannica Corporation, 1969.
$59.50
Grade level: 4-
Transparencies, teacher's manual, and student resource book presenting a
survey of the card catalog, reference books, dictionaries, and encyclopedias.

Library Skills for Primary Grades. St. Louis, Mo., Milliken, 1973.
$ 6.95
Grade level: K-3
A teacher's guide, twelve color transparencies, and twenty-four spirit masters
provide an introduction and practice in the care of materials, alphabetical
order, parts of a book, book arrangement, catalog cards, and reference books.

Library Transparencies. Maplewood, N.J., Hammond, 1969.
$57.00
Grade level: 4-8
Aids for the teaching of classification, arrangement of books, and the card
catalog.

Making Inferences from Maps. Redwood City, Calif., Visual Materials, Inc., 1971.
$ 6.95
Grade level: 5-
This set may be used for more detailed units on map study. Solving map
problems through inference is stressed.

Map Reading Skills. Redwood City, Calif., Visual Materials, Inc., 1971.
$ 6.95
Grade level: 3-5
Transparencies and spirit masters related to introductory map skills,
symbols, and terminology.

Outlining Skills. Redwood City, Calif., Visual Materials, Inc., 1971.
$ 6.95
Grade level: 5-
Introduces basic outline formats for reports and creative compositions.

Reference Tools and Study Skills. St. Louis, Mo., Milliken, 1972.
$ 6.95
Grade level: 4-8
The teacher's guide, twelve transparencies, and twenty-four spirit masters
introduce specific reference tools from dictionaries to textbooks and suggest
the most efficient use of these resources.

Using the Card Catalog. Chicago, Colonial Films, 1967.
$37.00
Grade level: 3-8

Eight color transparencies provide specific information on various details regarding the use of the card catalog.

Using the Card Catalog. Maplewood, N.J., Hammond, 1969.
$24.00
Grade level: 4-8
This accurate set of transparencies provides an introduction to the use of the card catalog.

Using the Dictionary. Redwood City, Calif., Visual Materials, Inc., 1971.
$ 6.95
Grade level: 5-8
The transparencies and spirit masters provide practice in basic dictionary skills, such as alphabetizing, guide words, and pronunciation keys.

Using the Library Instructional Materials Center Effectively. Big Springs, Tex., Creative Visuals, 1970.
$299.00
Grade level: 5-8
The color transparencies and teacher's guide introduce the Dewey Decimal arrangement, non-print materials, and specific reference books.

PRINT

(This is a title listing.)

A Book to Begin on Libraries, by Susan Bartlett. New York, Holt, Rinehart, and Winston, 1964.
$ 3.27
Grade level: 4-8
Introduction to the history and importance of books and libraries.

Books Lead the Way: A Related Library and Reading Skill Text, by Eileen Conlon. Metuchen, N.J., Scarecrow Press.
$ 4.25
Grade level: 6-
Exercise in print skills necessary for locating and using information.

Children's Book on How to Use Books and Libraries, by Carolyn Mott and Leo B. Baisden. New York, Scribner's, 1968.
$ 3.42
Grade level: 3-8
Book and workbook including elementary lessons on alphabetizing, the book, the Dewey Decimal System, dictionaries, encyclopedias, atlases, and the writing of book reviews.

Detecting the Sequence. Baldwin, N.Y., Dexter & Westbrook, Ltd., 1972.
$ 1.25 each
Grade level: 1-
Each booklet at reading levels one through six and advanced provides practice at a given level in specific sequencing skills.

Dictionary Skills, Volumes I–IV. Hueytown, Ala., Educational Services, 1975.
$ 5.25 each
Grade level: 3-
Each volume consists of forty spirit masters activities; covers all areas of dictionary skills.

Drawing Conclusions. Baldwin, N.Y., Dexter & Westbrook, Ltd., 1972.
$ 1.25 each
Grade level: 1-
Activities at each reading level (one through six) provide practice in drawing conclusions.

The Elementary School Library in Action, by Lora Palovic and Elizabeth Goodman. West Nyack, N.Y., Parker Publishing Co., 1968.
$ 8.95
Grade level: professional
This book provides helpful suggestions for library-oriented activities that might be adapted for teaching media skills within the subject areas.

The First Book of Facts and How to Find Them, by David C. Whitney. New York, Watts, 1966.
$ 3.45
Grade level: 2-6
This provides a guide to reference books and the parts of these books which are helpful.

Following Directions. Baldwin, N.Y., Dexter & Westbrook, Ltd., 1972.
$ 1.25 each
Grade level: 1-
Practice activities at each reading level provide practice in following directions.

Getting the Facts. Baldwin, N.Y., Dexter & Westbrook, Ltd., 1972.
$ 1.25 each
Grade level: 2-
Each booklet at a given reading level provides material from which students may practice finding facts.

Getting the Main Idea. Baldwin, N.Y., Dexter & Westbrook, Ltd., 1972.
$ 1.25 each
Grade level: 2-
The booklets (one through six) provide practice in identifying main ideas at given reading levels.

Graphs and Surveys. Middleton, Conn., Xerox.
$ 0.45
Grade level: 4-
Pamphlet presents basic information on the interpretation of graphs and surveys.

A Guidebook for Introducing Library Skills to Kindergarten and Primary Grades, by Margaret V. Beck and Vera M. Pace. Minneapolis, Minn., Denison, 1967.
$ 6.95
Grade level: K-1
Focuses on book appreciation and understanding the functions of a library.

A Guidebook for Teaching Library Skills, Book One, by Margaret V. Beck and Vera M. Pace. Minneapolis, Minn., Denison, 1965.
$ 6.95
Grade level: K-2
Deals primarily with the skills involved in using the card catalog. Includes activities aimed at motivating the use of the library.

A Guidebook for Teaching Library Skills—Book Two, by Margaret V. Beck and Vera M. Pace. Minneapolis, Minn., Denison, 1965.
$ 6.95
Grade level: 3-6
Provides for students a sequential series of practice exercises on the Dewey Decimal arrangement of materials.

A Guidebook for Teaching Library Skills—Book Three, by Margaret V. Beck and Vera M. Pace. Minneapolis, Minn., Denison, 1966.
$ 6.95
Grade level: 3-6
Emphasizes reference tools (e.g., the encyclopedia, almanac, atlas, biographical dictionary, and *Readers' Guide to Periodical Literature*) and simple research techniques.

A Guidebook for Teaching Library Skills—Book Four, by Marion L. Welken. Minneapolis, Minn., Denison, 1967.
$ 6.95
Grade level: 4-7
Includes an overview of the school library and provides activities related to the parts of books, library arrangement, the card catalog, encyclopedias, and reference books. Includes a test.

How Reference Resources Help Us, by William T. Nichol. Westchester, Ill.,
   Benefic Press, 1966.
   $ 4.25
   Grade level: 4-8
   Introduces a wide range of reference sources, both print and non-print.

How to Use the Library. Boston, Mass., Allyn and Bacon, Inc., 1966.
   $ 2.50
   Grade level: 5-
   This set, consisting of a teacher's manual, an exhibit book, and a program
   book, provides an individualized approach to library use.

How to Use the Readers' Guide to Periodical Literature. Bronx, N.Y., H. W.
   Wilson.
   Free
   Grade level: 6-
   This short booklet explains the purpose of the *Readers' Guide to Periodical
   Literature* and provides some practice questions.

Learning to Alphabetize and Using Guide Words. Baldwin, N.Y., Dexter & Westbrook, 1972.
   $26.95
   Grade level: 1-
   Exercises in both alphabetizing and use of guide words is provided for students at reading levels one through nine.

Learning to Use the Library. New York, Xerox.
   $ 0.35 each
   Grade level: 3-
   Book A deals with parts of a book.
   Book B includes games about the Dewey Decimal System.
   Book C teaches the use of the *Readers' Guide to Periodical Literature*.
   Book D covers specific reference sources.

Library Skills. Elizabethtown, Pa., Continental Press, 1967.
   $ 6.95
   Grade level: 3-7
   Contains spirit masters related to the parts of a book, book arrangement, the
   card catalog, and reference books. The teacher's guide provides suggested
   teaching procedures.

Locating the Answer. Baldwin, N.Y., Dexter & Westbrook, Ltd., 1972.
   $ 1.25 each
   Grade level: 2-
   Specific activities in booklets at seven reading levels provide practice in
   locating answers.

Look-It-Up Book 1. Chicago, Field Enterprises Educational Corporation.
$ 0.05
Grade level: 3-7
This pamphlet is designed to provide practice in beginning encyclopedia skills.

Look-It-Up Book 2. Chicago, Field Enterprises Educational Corporation.
$ 0.05
Grade level: 4-7
After a short review, the pamphlet provides practice in the more complicated skills involved in the use of the encyclopedia.

Map Skills for Today. New York, Xerox.
$ 0.35
Grade level: 3-
Five sequential books, progressing from primary to intermediate map skills.

Open the Book, by Roberta Bishop Freund. Metuchen, N.J., Scarecrow Press, 1966.
$ 6.00
Grade level: 3-8
Sample lessons and lesson plans on the card catalog, encyclopedias, reference sources, bibliographies, and notetaking.

Practice in Dictionary Skills. Duluth, Minn., Instructor Publications, 1973.
$ 3.95
Grade level: 3-7
Practice in specific dictionary skills, such as dealing with multiple meanings, identifying the schwa, etc.

Practice in Library Skills. Duluth, Minn., Instructor Publications, 1973.
$ 4.00
Grade level: 5-8
The twenty-four spirit masters serve as practice sheets for such topics as book arrangement, card catalog, the Dewey Decimal System, parts of a book, dictionaries, encyclopedias, reference books, microfilm, audiovisual materials, and notetaking.

Practice in Research and Study Skills. Duluth, Minn., Instructor Publications, 1974
$ 3.95 each
Grade level: 4-8
Each spirit master book (A, B, and C) provides practice sheets for specific study skills.

Stepping Stones to the Library. Bronx, N.Y., Fordham Equipment and Publishing
　　Co., 1972.
　　$ 6.95
　　Grade level: K-3
　　Spirit masters provide "fun" puzzles and activities to teach beginning media
　　skills.

Study Skills for Information Retrieval. Boston, Mass., Allyn and Bacon, 1970.
　　$ 1.95 each
　　Grade level: 2-8
　　Series provides in-depth exercises in such areas as alphabetizing, dictionaries,
　　parts of a book, encyclopedias, library use, maps, charts, graphs, and report
　　writing (books one through four).

Table and Graph Skills. New York, Xerox, 1975.
　　$ 0.40
　　Grade level: 3-6
　　Includes exercises in the vocabulary of graphs, solving problems with graphs,
　　kinds of graphs, and interpretation of graphs (Books A through D).

Teaching Study Skills. Duluth, Minn., Instructor Publications, 1973.
　　$ 1.50
　　Grade level: 4-
　　Gives ideas for presenting study skills to students.

Using a Table of Contents. Baldwin, N.Y., Dexter & Westbrook, Ltd., 1972.
　　$ 9.95
　　Grade level: 1-
　　Practice exercises in using a table of contents at given reading levels (books
　　one through nine).

Using an Index. Baldwin, N.Y., Dexter & Westbrook, Ltd., 1972.
　　$12.95
　　Grade level: 3-7
　　Booklets are designed to develop indexing skills at specific reading levels.

Using the Dik-shuh-nair-ee. New York, Xerox, 1973.
　　$ 0.35
　　Grade level: 4-6
　　The series of four books (Books A, B, C, and D) may be used with any
　　standard dictionary. Proceeds from simple alphabetizing to vowel sounds.

PART IV—LIST OF VENDORS

ACI Films
35 W. 45th Street
New York, N.Y. 10036

Allyn and Bacon, Inc.
470 Atlantic Avenue
Boston, Mass. 02210

Audio-Education, Inc.
3134 Sawtelle Boulevard
Los Angeles, Calif. 90066

Benefic Press
10300 W. Roosevelt Road
Westchester, Ill. 60153

BFA Educational Media
Division of CBS
2211 Michigan Avenue
Santa Monica, Calif. 90404

Bro-Dart, Inc.
Eastern Division
1609 Memorial Avenue
Williamsport, Pa. 17701

or

Western Division
15255 E. Don Julian Road
City of Industry, Calif. 91749

Children's Book Council, Inc.
67 Irving Place
New York, N.Y. 10003

Colonial Films
752 Spring Street, N.W.
Atlanta, Ga. 30308

Continental Press, Inc.
Elizabethtown, Pa. 17022

Creative Visuals
Box 1911
Big Springs, Tex. 79720

T. S. Denison & Co., Inc.
321 Fifth Avenue, S.
Minneapolis, Minn. 55415

Denoyer Geppert Co.
Subs. of Times Mirror Co.
5235 Ravenswood Avenue
Chicago, Ill. 60640

Dexter & Westbrook, Ltd.
958 Church Street
Baldwin, N.Y. 11510

Educational Insights
Dept. T
211 S. Hindry Avenue
Inglewood, Calif. 90301

Educational Filmstrips
1401 9th Street
Huntsville, Tex. 77340

Educational Services
P.O. Box 3130
Hueytown, Ala. 35020

Encyclopaedia Britannica Educational Corporation
425 N. Michigan Avenue
Chicago, Ill. 60611

Eye-Gate House
146-01 Archer Avenue
Jamaica, N.Y. 11435

Field Enterprises Educational
  Corporation
510 Merchandise Mart Plaza
Chicago, Ill. 60654

Filmstrip House, Inc.
432 Park Avenue South
New York, N.Y. 10016

Fordham Equipment and Publishing Company
2377 Hoffman Street
Bronx, N.Y. 10458

Gaylord Brothers, Inc.
Box 61
Syracuse, N.Y. 13201

or

Box 8489
Stockton, Calif. 95204

Hammond Incorporated
515 Valley Street
Maplewood, N.J. 07040

Holt, Rinehart, and Winston
383 Madison Avenue
New York, N.Y. 10017

Ideal School Supply
11000 S. La Vergne Avenue
Oak Lawn, Ill. 60453

Imperial Educational Resources
4900 South Lewis Avenue
P.O. Box 7068
Tulsa, Okla. 74105

Instructo Corporation
Paoli, Pa. 19301

Instructor Publications
P.O. Box 6108
Duluth, Minn. 55806

Learning Systems Co.
60 Connolly Parkway
Hamden, Conn. 06514

Library Filmstrip Center
3033 Aloma
Wichita, Kans. 67211

Long Filmslide Service
7505 Fairmount Avenue
El Cerrito, Calif. 94530

McGraw-Hill Films
330 W. 42nd Street
New York, N.Y. 10036

Media Materials, Inc.
409 West Cold Spring Lane
Baltimore, Md. 21210

Milliken Publishing Company
611 Olive Street
St. Louis, Miss. 63101

National Geographic Society
17th and M Streets, N.W.
Washington, D.C. 20036

Nifty Division
St. Regis Paper Company
3300 Pinson Valley Parkway
Birmingham, Ala. 35217

Nystrom, A. J. & Co.
3333 Elston Avenue
Chicago, Ill. 60618

Pacific Productions
Educational Film Division
2614 Etna Street
Berkeley, Calif. 94704

Parker Publishing Company
West Nyack, N.Y. 10994

Pied Piper Productions
P.O. Box 320
Verdugo City, Calif. 91406

Prentice-Hall, Inc.
70 5th Avenue
New York, N.Y. 10011

Scarecrow Press, Inc.
52 Liberty Street
Metuchen, N.J. 18840

Warren Schloat Productions
115 Tompkins Avenue
Pleasantville, N.Y. 10570

Science Research Associates
259 E. Erie Street
Chicago, Ill. 60611

Charles Scribner's Sons
597 Fifth Avenue
New York, N.Y. 10017

Society for Visual Education, Inc.
1345 Diversey Parkway
Chicago, Ill. 60614

Sturgis Library Products
P.O. Box 130
Sturgis, Mich. 49091

Troll Associates
320 Route 17
Mahwah, N.J. 07430

Visual Materials, Inc.
2549 Middlefield Road
Redwood City, Calif. 94063

Franklin Watts, Inc.
575 Lexington Avenue
New York, N.Y. 10022

H. W. Wilson Co.
950 University Avenue
Bronx, N.Y. 10452

Wollensak Teaching Tapes
3M Co.
Mincom Division
3M Center
St. Paul, Minn. 55101

Xerox Education Publications
245 Long Hill Road
Middleton, Conn. 06457

INDEX

Accountability, 9, 27
Administrators
  role in implementing media skills program,
    70-72, 76-77
    See also Principal.
Almanacs
  lessons related to, 136-138, 149-153, 157-159
Alphabetizing skills
  lessons related to, 14-21, 43, 48-55, 85-88
Animals
  media skills lessons related to, 14-21, 42,
    104-105, 116-123
Appendix
  lessons related to, 133-134
Application skills
  K-8 sequence, 34-35
April Fool's Day. *See* Holidays.
Art
  media skills lessons related to, 90-91, 96-97
Assessment. *See* Tests and testing.
Atlases
  lessons related to, 140, 149-153
Audiovisual equipment
  lessons related to, 91-93, 112-116, 122-
    127, 131, 135, 139-140, 143, 148-153,
    155-156
    See also Audiovisual instruction.
Audiovisual instruction
  definition, 43
  lessons related to, 43, 112-113, 126-127,
    143
Authors and illustrators
  lessons related to, 90-91

Biography
  lessons related to, 105-106
Black Americans
  media skills lessons related to, 127-128

Card catalog
  lessons related to, 43, 60, 108, 148-153
Career education
  media skills lessons related to, 97-98
Catalog cards. *See* Card catalog.
Characters, fictional
  lessons related to, 141-142
Christmas. *See* Holidays.
Cities
  media skills lessons related to, 89-90,
    154-157
Civil War
  media skills lessons related to, 60

Committee, media skills, 72
Communications
  media skills lessons related to, 128-130
Community
  variables related to, 44, 47, 51, 53
  media skills lessons related to, 130-131
Comprehension skills
  as a media skills program objective, 25, 29
  K-8 sequence, 34-35
Contracting
  examples related to, 53, 55
Curriculum
  variables related to, 46, 48, 49
  integration of media skills into, 72

Decimals and fractions
  media skills lessons related to, 100-103
Decoding
  lessons related to, 154
Deductive approach, 44
Demonstration method of instruction
  definition, 42
  examples, 42-43, 155-156
Development activities, 60
Dewey Decimal System
  lessons related to, 100-103
Dictionaries
  lessons related to, 48-55, 85, 88, 98-100,
    105-106, 144-145
Dinosaurs
  media skills lessons related to, 147
Discussion method of instruction
  definition, 42
  examples, 42, 55, 107, 128-129, 132, 138-
    139, 141-142, 154
Drill method of instruction
  definition, 43
  examples, 43, 97-98, 100-101
Drymount press. *See* Audiovisual equipment.

Ecology
  media skills lessons related to, 119-122
Economics
  media skills lessons related to, 132
Egypt, ancient
  media skills lessons related to, 132-134
Encyclopedias
  lessons related to, 117, 122-123, 128-130,
    136-138, 141, 143-145, 149-153
Evaluation. *See* Tests and testing.
Explorers
  media skills lessons related to, 43
Expository approach, 44

185

Media production skills
  examples of lessons related to, 14-21, 42
  as a media skills program objective, 25, 29
  K-8 sequence, 37-38
    See also Audiovisual equipment; Audio-
    visual instruction; Filmstrips; Slides.
Methods of instruction
  variables related to, 46, 48-55, 61
    See also under specific methods (e.g.,
    Lecture method of instruction).
Model, instructional
  general, 12-13
  for media skills, 21-23
Mother's Day. *See* Holidays.
Music
  media skills lessons related to, 103-104
Mythology
  media skills lessons related to, 39, 113-114,
    138-139
    See also Greece, ancient.

Newspapers
  lessons related to, 113, 130-131, 136-138
Notes and notetaking
  lessons related to, 142-143

Objectives. *See* Objectives, instructional;
  Objectives, performance; Objectives,
  program.
Objectives, general educational. *See* Objectives,
  program.
Objectives, instructional
  in teaching model, 12-13
  integration of media skills into classroom,
    13-14, 40
  in media skills model, 21-23
  and accountability, 27
  definition, 27, 40
  examples, 27, 49, 54, 85, 89-91, 93, 96-
    98, 100, 102-108, 110-114, 116-117,
    119, 122-133, 135-136, 138-145, 147-
    149, 153-157
  function of, 27, 40
  relation to learning activities, 27
  relation to observable student performance,
    27
  relation to student behavior, 27, 40
  distinguished from performance and
    program objectives, 28, 39-40
  sequence for media skills, 28-38
  and units, 40, 56
Objectives, performance
  compared to program and instructional
    objectives, 39, 40
  definition, 28, 40
  described by Robert Mager, 29
  distinguished from instructional objec-
    tives, 28, 39-40

Objectives, performance (cont'd)
  examples, 28, 59
  in lesson planning, 59
  writing of, 29, 39
    See also Objectives, instructional.
Objectives, program
  and cultural values, 25
  compared to instructional and performance
    objectives, 39
  definition, 25
  described by Benjamin Bloom, 26
  for media skills, 25-27
  function of, 25, 39
Organization, school
  variables related to, 46-47, 49-51, 53

Performance objectives. *See* Objectives,
  performance.
Periodicals
  lessons related to, 127-128, 130-131
Pets
  media skills lessons related to, 122-123
Physical education
  media skills lessons related to, 89
Planning, instructional
  media specialist and teacher, 13-14
  and media skills objectives, 28
  of units, 55-59
  and content, 56, 61
  and pre-testing, 56, 61
  and resources, 56, 61
  and unit objectives, 56, 61
  and instructional responsibilities, 57, 61
  and student groupings, 57-58, 61
  and unit strategies, 57, 61
  and allocation of time, 58, 61
  and selection of resources, 58, 61
  and testing, 58, 61
  of lessons, 59-61
    See also Media specialist; Teachers.
Plants
  media skills lessons related to, 124
Plot
  lessons related to, 89-90, 107
Poetry
  media skills lessons related to, 114-116
Practice method of instruction
  definition, 43
  examples, 43, 100-101, 104-106, 108-109,
    117-119, 133-134, 138-140, 142-146,
    148, 155-159
Pre-tests and pre-testing
  examples, 15-16, 52, 54
  general description of, 56
    See also Tests and testing.
Prediction
  lessons related to, 112
Prehistoric animals
  media skills lessons related to, 147